The Life of the Soul

Samuel H. Miller

There is in this book a genuine spiritual adventure waiting for the reader who will discover it.

Few contemporary writers have been able to set forth the life of the human soul in the Christian tradition with such simple beauty of phrase and such penetrating insight into its illusions, predicaments, hopes, and ultimate realizations.

Books cannot discover God for man, as Dr. Miller admits. But they may show man his need for God, his helplessness without Him, his estrangement from mankind apart from Him, and the peace and joy of realization of Him. All this THE LIFE OF THE SOUL does, and more, in old ideas newly expressed, in thought clear and compelling and in language memorable and distinguished.

Samuel Miller (deceased) was for many years the Dean of the Harvard Divinity School, and the author of a number of books.

THE LIFE OF THE SOUL

THE LIFE OF THE SOUL

Samuel H. Miller

Phoenix Press

WALKER AND COMPANY
New York

Large Print Edition published by arrangement with Franklin William Miller and Myra Miller Bryan

Copyright, 1951, by Harper & Brothers

Photoset by Rowland Phototypesetting Ltd, Bury St Edmunds, Suffolk, England.

Printed in the United States of America.

Library of Congress Cataloging in Publication Data

Miller, Samuel Howard, 1900–
　The life of the soul.

　1. Soul. 2. Spiritual life. 3. Large type books.
I. Title.
BT741.2.M56　1986　　　　233'.5　　　　　86-13360
ISBN 0-8027-2551-1 (lg. print)

10 9 8 7 6 5 4 3 2 1

First Large Print Edition, 1986
Walker and Company
720 Fifth Avenue
New York, NY 10019

Contents

1. The Career of the Soul — 1
2. The Dread of Religion — 16
3. On Coming to Oneself — 28
4. Soul and Society — 43
5. Loneliness and God — 57
6. The Singular Decision — 68
7. The Eternal and Its Substitutes — 78
8. Spiritual Health — 91
9. Hiding Places of Power — 104
10. The Realm of Peace — 118
11. Dealing with Spiritual Slackness — 131
12. Prayer and Life — 143
13. The Travail of Glory — 153
14. The Inevitable Cross — 169
15. Beginning Eternity Now — 182

THE LIFE OF THE SOUL

1

The Career of the Soul

THERE is a great deal of mystery in a human life; so much indeed that we prefer to hide the depth of it from ourselves and others by many devices. Between birth and death, the years are filled with the innumerable problems of growing up, of failure and folly, of achievement and hope, of joy and desire, endlessly changing from hour to hour, but always pointing a question at our puzzled brains—What can be made of this? or Why did it come my way? or What will come of it in time? There are turns and twists, low places and high, rough and easy, some places full of peace and others of battles, a few glorified by vision and understanding, and many confused by the uproar of the world's opinions. My life—there it is—climbing through the hours from dawn till dark, struggling invisibly, seeking, failing, hoping, hiding its pain, trying with blundering hands to bless someone or something, and always and everywhere not a little baffled! What can anyone make of it? It is so full of fits and starts, of barren spaces and erratic fires, of incommensurable dreams and tragic carelessness.

Well, someday it is supposed to be a soul for God!

But what is the soul? Where in this tenement of bone, windowed with the senses, does it dwell? Are the smells and sights and touch of the world a part of it, or is there an endless enmity between the body born of the flesh, and the soul born of the spirit? How does the soul come to be? What happens to this troubled handful of dust, breathing, snarling, dreaming, that it should ponder on questions of eternal destiny and claim within itself something immortal? From the hidden but not unrecorded experiences of infancy, from the flashes of likes and dislikes of childhood, from terror and shame and ecstasy, from revelations bright with irresistible glory, from all manner of circumstance, humble, ephemeral, crude, delightful, vague, the soul begins to take its shape and color. From the familiar tree in the yard, from the red kite, from the memory of death, from the bitter lash of scorn, from the seed of truth rooting itself in the brain—from such casual mysteries the soul takes its garments.

Somewhere out of life, out of all its multitudinous items, out of the broad river of our existence, flowing between the banks of this human clay, out of thoughts and deeds and the mere shadow of thoughts and deeds, out of pain and hope and fear and desire, the soul is born—born of the will of God, mysteriously, wondrously, with the wings of an inevitable destiny known only in God's dreaming.

Yet in the realm of religion there are many who feel that the soul is not at all subject to the necessities of growing pains and a long struggle to maturity. For them the soul is something unchangeable, equally possessed by all human beings. It is the inevitable accompaniment of the human body, having been given by God at birth or before, and guaranteeing life after death. It is a kind of check, made payable to the bearer in terms of salvation and immortality. All one needs to do to endorse the check and enjoy its promise is to join the Church, or to believe in God, or to be morally decent. That notion thinks of the soul as static, unchangeable, the possession once and for all of man.

For others, however, it is not static, but dynamic. It is not unchangeable, but full of possibilities. It is not only born, but growing, maturing, failing and succeeding, achieving skill and insight, or lapsing into darkness, confusion and sin. Just as the brain may be trained, so may the soul be trained. Just as there is a world of information and truth for the brain to learn, so there is a realm of spiritual wisdom for the soul to understand and practice. Just as there are countless fumbling actions for the body to repeat before the muscles learn the simplest skills of walking and talking, not to speak of the higher arts and crafts, so there are innumerable actions necessary for the soul to practice before it moves freely and with graceful power among life's bedlam of circumstance.

If one scans the situation, it is evident that many people live on the basis of the first notion. They are anxious for the soul to be acknowledged, for the check to be cashed for the Church to be joined, but having done these things, the whole matter is concluded. They have fulfilled the requirements and all is finished. Indeed, too often in the Protestant church the birth of the soul into conscious spiritual life, symbolized by baptism, has become the very climax of Christian desire and attention, with the result that many scarcely enter the Church before they go slack, their souls drop off to sleep, and their spiritual energies stagnate or atrophy. They are in truth stillborn souls.

Jesus tells the story of this multitude in brief but unforgettable phrases. They began to build but were unable to finish. They built the basement and then quickly and easily satisfied, counted it foolish to continue their labor. For the rest of their lives they proudly inhabited what was meant only for a beginning and in time forgot that there was ever to be anything more. These "minimumites" preferring basements to cathedrals, living on the first impulse of religion and making it stretch over a whole lifetime, embalming the past and substituting it for the present—these are the Church's greatest problem. They count it Christian loyalty to cling to the infantile notions with which they began their religious life, whereas, it might better be called arrested development, if not downright stupidity.

One comes to realize that this was one of the reasons why Jesus ruthlessly demanded so much of his followers. Multitudes were crowding his meetings, shouting his name, and praising him in extravagant terms. Plenty of them were willing to begin their discipleship, but they had no thought of how hard it would become after the novelty wore off and the demonstrations ceased, after the popularity waned and the persecution began, and the Cross loomed up and doubts took root. Jesus, therefore, ruthlessly, cruelly, pushed these "easy starters" back against the wall of such rigorous demands that they had to make decisions which would carry them out and away from everything they had known. Hate your family, leave your holdings, forget your reputation, sell everything—if you want to follow me, you must follow one who has no place to lay his head, who leads a pilgrim life, and because growing is suffering, you must take up your cross, not merely for a beginning, but for all time. It is easy enough to begin a thing, no matter how difficult it is or how superficial we are, but it is a different matter to continue through a long discipline until it is concluded creatively.

Of all things do not let us think that here we are talking about other people. We are talking about ourselves. One of the severest problems met by any Christian is the question of his growth in the wisdom of the gospel. Even our physical bodies are a mystery to us—can we by taking thought add one cubit to our stature? And our mental growth is far from a simple matter easily estimated and prescribed. How much more perplexing then is the realm of the soul, of love and sin and repentance and God and creation. How does a soul grow? How can we increase our knowledge of God and His ways? You and I and all others have been building basements, or a little more—but how shall we build cathedral souls? There is no more baffling and subtle art than the training of the soul.

Let us look at the matter quite practically. There are two facts which we cannot miss if we sincerely seek to bring our souls to maturity. First of all there is a vast field of spiritual wisdom waiting to be pondered and understood. It is just as essentially spiritual as the field of intellectual truth is rational. The two are not the same, any more than faith is reason. That field of religious wisdom was penetratingly revealed and vividly demonstrated by Jesus in his teachings and in his actions. It remains in the New Testament as the gospel. It is the very formula of eternal things and divine things and divine activities. Our first step is to be imaginatively aware of the wisdom that is available for the soul's nurture.

The second fact is as plain as the first. One must practice the doing of things even before one knows how to do them. As impossible as that sounds, it is the simple necessity of learning in any art or craft. We have to cook before we know how to cook. We have to hammer and saw, clumsily and with grotesque results, before we can become a carpenter. We have to stumble and fall if we are to walk. The only way in which we can grow into something better than we are now is to do things we are not strictly able to do. We will have to subject ourselves to certain disciplines, the practice of exercises, which we will not do well at first, and which will, therefore, inevitably embarrass and disappoint us. It will take a great deal of failing before we accomplish the satisfactions of a skillful soul, creative in its own original insights and freedom of action.

Moreover, there are certain traditional disciplines for the training of the soul which would not need to be mentioned except that they have fallen into neglect and abuse. Take for instance Bible reading, prayer and the Church. Bible reading can and does degenerate into the stuffiest and stalest routine on earth, but when it is done by those who know why they are reading and what they are looking for, when it is the fascinating exploration of a great field of spiritual wisdom, revealed and made vivid by life and action, then it rises to a high creative act in the training of the soul. Similarly, prayer can become as flat and tasteless as a stock report, but when it is real it is the vantage point from which we see with fearless wide-open eyes the full panorama of our lives inter-tangled with one another, the world and God, and see it all in the light of the grand design of God's kingdom so that we are able to survey the situation of our soul and definitely set about the reformation of its habits.

In like manner the Church may drop from its destined function until it becomes only a dead weight for man to carry, a heavy burden, an aggravation to anyone with honesty and vigor of life in head or heart. But if the Church is what it ought to be, it will rise as the spontaneous fellowship of men and women, a winged and buoyant comradeship, fascinated by the lure of spiritual wisdom and its creative practice. These traditional disciplines have been so heavily encrusted with bad habits and unwise usage, that every one of them bores people to death instead of giving them life. They ought to be the very music of God's kingdom, with a lift and a lilt to inspire. They ought to be windows and gateways, but all too often prove insurmountable barricades. If we are going to use them, in the name of our souls, let us not use them blindly but make them serve the creative purpose of our souls.

With the obvious traditional disciplines of worship and prayer there are certain primary attitudes essential to even the most elementary progress in spiritual living. Here one will be called upon to experiment with the very nature of the gospel and its way of life. None of these things will seem startling, but quite the reverse.

First of all we must stop protecting ourselves. We lock not only the doors of our houses in fear, but our souls as well. We are not only suspicious of strangers, but we keep our friends at arm's length. We are afraid to let our souls play. We are cautious lest we be taken for fools. We are on guard lest we be surprised. We keep the checkreins taut upon our souls lest they carry us beyond ourselves. We fear too much joy; our laughter is uncertain; our affection hesitates. We open our hand but our heart is covered. Our pride holds us back from life, strange in its newness, lest it be embarrassed. We are anxious about the future and, therefore, we cannot enjoy the present. Our reputation teaches us to see nothing but the outside of people, lest their souls see ours. We fear failure more than we love life, so we refuse the great ventures. We are careful to do only what we have always done and know how to do well, so we never break the dull repetition of the old routine for the new creation in God. Crawl out of these tombs and prisons—there is a world of light and freedom waiting! Have faith in God and let life be free. Stop riding the brakes on the heart. The soul will never grow, tied down in bed, with the shades drawn. The higher and more secure we build the barricades of care and caution to protect ourselves, the deeper grows the grave we call our life.

But isn't there danger in this? Certainly! We will have trouble just as Jesus did, and the disciples, martyrs and saints after him. People will take advantage of us, and those who call themselves sensible will laugh at us behind our back and smile at us before our face. But it is better, as Jesus remarked, to run the risk and get into life with a broken leg, or a crippled arm, or a blind eye, or any other injury or misfortune, than to exist in the cramped dimensions of the dead, measured in fear and self-concern, to be fit at last only for the rubbish heaps outside creation's walls. You can make your choice, take it or leave it, but the soul will only grow in freedom, perilous as the way may be. That is part of the mystery of God's allowance of evil. After all, we know that the soul lives by faith, and what is faith but the daring to live without self-concern.

The second suggestion is to hold humble things in reverence. I realize how prone we are to be awed by the spectacular and the novel, to believe in miracles rather than in God, to grovel before success, to honor the influential and to respect the powerful. I know the more usual a thing is the blinder we become to it, and take for granted that we understand it inside and out. I know that pride feeds on sight of power, so that it is more difficult to see glory in a blade of grass than in a flaming comet.

Yet I also know that the Eternal Word became flesh, entered into the narrow alley of time, because man easily misunderstood, quickly persecuted, misjudged and roughly put to death. God always humbles Himself, travelling in this world incognito, now in the burning bush, now a voice in the night, now the potter's wheel, now the lowly Carpenter of Nazareth, now the blinding light of the road to Damascus—He is the great Casual, passing us a thousand times a day in the crowded streets of circumstance and always in a different guise, the eternal One of infinite resource. How easy it must have been for his neighbors to think of Jesus as merely another carpenter with a few strange and startling notions and a disturbing way of living. God humbles Himself so we may enjoy Him, and we exhalt ourselves so that we can reach Him—and thus we miss Him. Like faith, humility is also the life of the soul, and what is humility but holding common things, and unpretentious people, and ordinary events in reverence?

The third suggestion is to let your soul speak for itself. Some souls hold conversation with God in music, and some in the sowing of seed, and others in the smell of sawed wood, and still others in the affectionate understanding of their friends. All souls are not alike. Utter your own prayer, in the language of your own joy. Repent of your own sin and let your lament be your own sorrow and not another's. When you worship, thank God for whatever has given you joy, though it be so slight that no other soul would think it worthy of mention. Let your own insights sing their praise of creation, and your own handiwork adore the Invisible Creator. Quit dressing your soul in somebody else's piety. Your soul is not a pauper. Let it live its own life. Truth is just as necessary for the life of the soul as faith and humility, and truth is not merely the final and authoritative statement of the universe's wide design or life's deepest meaning—no, truth is the soul being itself.

If then you have begun to build, remember that beginning is not enough. Take upon yourself the disciplines of growth; live freely and in faith; keep your eyes alert and your soul humble that you may not miss the visit of the eternal in your neighborhood of circumstance and experience. Most of all, untie your soul, give it room to breathe, let it play, do not be ashamed of it. It is the child of the eternal and destined for greater things than you dream.

2

The Dread of Religion

WE will not go far in the search for the soul before we discover a peculiar resistance in us. There will be strange tactics of elusive and evasive action, and even hostile threats and stubbornness. Any permanent dynamic in spiritual progress will depend largely on how courageously we search out these hidden hindrances and subtle fears.

All of us know that there are things in our hearts which we are slow to admit, even to ourselves. Some of the things we have done or thought, instinctively or in spite of ourselves, we prefer to conceal, sometimes consciously, sometimes unconsciously. We have attics and cellars in our souls where we put the experiences we do not wish our friends to see, and deeper darknesses where we drop the experiences we ourselves desire to forget. And we are singularly cunning in this business of forgetting. We have experiences to which we take such a violent dislike, that we put them from us so quickly that we may never recall having had them.

I should like to say that we have all had a dread of religion, but I presume that many of us will immediately say that we cannot recall any such reaction. We may confess that there are certain kinds of religion which we dislike but that is nothing to conceal. We may have been disgusted with the emotional perversions and vulgarities of a certain sect, or repelled by the bombast of noisy Pharisees; the little squeamish "mousiness" of some people, or the presumptuous busybodying of others may have been deeply repugnant, but to dread religion—why, of course not! We were brought up in Christian homes, attended church and Sunday school. We believe in God and altogether look to religion as one of life's most inspiring resources. In fact, why should anyone dread religion? Its general appearance gives little indication of danger or disgrace lurking in it; a great deal of it at least seems quite consoling and rather harmless!

Yet I do not hesitate to press the point!

I believe that all of us can recover from our unidentified experiences (those from which we turned our eyes while they were happening and thereafter ignored) a real dread of religion. But because it is easier to see it in others before we see it in ourselves, let us lift our eyes from our own souls and listen to the testimony of men whose experience is undoubted. Here is Francis Thompson, poet extra-ordinary, telling of his dread in *The Hound of Heaven*. He fled from God "down the nights and down the days; . . . down the labyrinthine ways" of his own mind. With desperate haste and frantic hope he sought the security and refuge of Nature, then of human fellowship, and then of love, but all in vain. With mounting fear he waited blindly for the stroke of his relentless pursuer. He dreaded God, the "hound" of heaven.

Or turn to St. Augustine and read in his *Confessions* the moving story of how he strove by every strategy of a brilliant mind to steer clear of religion. From rhetoric to philosophy, from philosophy to passion and back again, until every escape cut off, he surrendered at last to what he once had feared.

Or look at the Gadarenes and the people of Nazareth, driving Jesus from their towns. Do not think it was merely because of radical views. It was because this Man's religion, the full power of it, demanded a yes-or-no decision from them, and evasions or compromise was impossible. The demons, who expressed what normal men would not allow themselves to say, spoke truth when they lashed out in hatred of the Christ.

It was when Peter saw the miraculous haul of fishes that he felt the tremendous awesomeness of Christ's mysteriously compelling spirit, and shouted hysterically at him: "Depart from me, get away, I'm sinful!"

Every one of the prophets utters his plea to God to spare him the awful intimacy of direct relationship with Him and His commands. They all deny their ability, they offer excuses, they ask for mercy, they cry to be delivered. To them the "fear of God" was not a rhetorical phrase, nor was it fear of God's wrath and injustice, as we superficial moderns would like to make it. It was the same fear of God which moved Cromwell to mumble on his death-bed, as he lay thinking of the way he had been guided into the responsibility of a destiny larger than he had ever dreamed or would have dared to take upon himself: "It is an awful thing to fall into the hands of the living God." Three times he uttered the words, and a lifetime of struggling with the stubborn circumstances of the world as a servant of the Most High was in them. So the ancient Jew feared God, and dared to say that this very dread, not of His wrath or of His injustice, but of His reality and power, was the beginning of all wisdom.

I press the point again! Even as the Israelites gathered on the slopes of Sinai besought Moses to go up and speak with God, but "let us not come nigh unto him, lest we die," so you and I wish to be somewhere in the circle of religion, counted among the friends of God, but not at the awful center where the naked soul confronts Eternal God. There is too much power there, too much light, too much fire —we cannot stand it, or resist it, or endure it. Look how hard it is to talk about God, even to our nearest friends. We are apt to be ill at ease, our hearts a little frightened. See how we evade religious conversations. There is something disturbing about them. We prefer not to meet religious matters head-on, but rather obliquely and somewhat casually. We sidestep courteously, nod and pass on quickly, hoping that we will not have to stop and talk. We are like boys in the presence of the neighborhood bully. We do not want to get too close, but we are careful not to appear hostile; we may even go out of our way to show how friendly we are, but when we do we keep him at arm's length, and breathe freer when he is not around. It is even so with religion and God. We inwardly dread them, but we make sure to appear, even to ourselves, as the very epitome of friendliness!

Now it is not at all meaningless that we should dread to meet religion head-on. The heart knows reasons where-of the brain is quite ignorant. Religion drives clean through every defense into the embarrassing privacy of the sensitive self. There are no secrets left. Every closet is opened, every drawer ransacked, every darkness explored. With a quiet but ruthless persistence, our inner life is uncovered, put out in plain sight where we cannot miss it, held up and our eyes held open. The shameful contradictions, the impulsive meannesses, the deliberate deceptions are all dragged out. It points out what we would like to forget—the scars of our hate, the slow smother of our indifference, the silent, irrevocable passing of time, the ghastly hollowness of our prayerless souls, the ugly altars to ourself, the long destiny of a thoughtless deed, the bitter fruit of caution, the vacant years, the lunatic lust for place and possession, the empty eye and the grasping hand, and all other acts and thoughts in which we did the devil's will, though we thought it our own. There is nothing hidden that shall not be revealed was the word of Jesus. And that is the reason we prefer to nod and pass on quickly, lest we be caught and probed by the finger of God.

Moreover, religion overwhelms us with breathless mysteries, and leaves us tangled in the midst of infinite paradoxes and mighty contradictions. It chants through every hour of slipping time, "In the beginning God created the heaven and the earth . . . and God said, Let there be light . . . and he divided it from the darkness. . . . And God created man in his own image; in the image of God, created he him; male and female created he them." The years will pass as a tale that is told and the vestments of the heavens will be changed, but God shall be forever, and at the end of all things He shall sit upon the throne and judge the earth. Creation and judgment, dim beginning and distant end, the long design of providence, birth and death, body and soul—thus the pattern is woven on a loom larger than our sight, in vast and solemn mysteries of pain and ecstasy, of dreams beyond the height of night and day, and deeds of inexpressible tenderness. Religion shakes down the walls of every partition, tears us from our isolation, rolls back the skies and leaves us standing before the unanswerable and unutterable mysteries of being. It opens our eyes to see the awful heights and depths, the hell and heaven of common circumstance and its consequence. It tears the veil from time and reveals the blinding splendor of eternity—there is no place here to lay your head, for the sight will take your breath away and leave your eyes hungry for a more comfortable darkness. The spirit searcheth the deep things of God, said Paul. No wonder you and I draw back!

It is also true that religion with a quiet but irresistible gesture sweeps the anxieties and ambitions and reputations of this world into oblivion before our very eyes. The things we labored so frantically to possess and now grasp so tightly and competently, fall by their own weight when the voice is heard nearer than breathing and plainer than pain, "This night thy soul shall be required of thee." O fool, to place such years of toil, so much mortal anguish, such longing and such splendor in things you will never get through the gate of death. So many frantic years, so many anxious nights, so many bargains and tricks, so many little advantages and so many bulging barns, so much ambition for such brief possession. Religion says, "Lay up treasures where moth and rust doth not corrupt, and thieves do not break through and steal." Yet in credulity we lean on all the props the earth affords. We lean upon the world, but it shifts from day to day, so that yesterday's strength is tomorrow's weakness. We count upon time, but we have only this fragile moment and a hope, and both may come to a sudden end. We look to pleasure, but it soon turns to a flat taste of despair. We straighten our backbone, stiffen our chin, and count on ourselves, but how presumptuous for such a changeable creature, now this now that, good and also evil, stretched upon the rack of many opposites, the victim of freedom, torn by incompatible desires. It is as if we were a host of varied shadows, with power to become each one in succession—what a strange uneven procession of inconsistent sincerities . . . . "Who shall deliver me from the body of this death?" cried Paul. No wonder we seek to busy ourselves with less disturbing considerations than religion.

Need I press the point now? Or argue the truth? We fear religion, the power of religion, and the revelations of religion. We are afraid of what God might do, afraid that if we let the door of our soul open, He would ride our will without consent or desire. We want to keep our hands upon the reins, to have the "say-so" of our life, to practice the sovereignty of our freedom, to turn to the right or left, to dabble and play, to follow no path or strive to no end. The power of God is an overwhelming thing. It created the universe; it upholds it; it shall judge it. See what it did to the man of Nazareth who was always saying, "Lose yourself," until he hung upon the Cross. See what it did to Paul who preached that the power of God was like an explosive, until carried away he lost his life. See what martyrs it has made, what fools of Christ. We do not fear the injustice of God, nor even His justice, but consciously or unconsciously we do everything we can to evade His power getting hold of us. It might be the end of us . . . yet . . . who knows, that may also mean the beginning of a new creation.

I rest the case now. What we dreaded would have been a new life had we accepted. What we resisted would have been a destiny for our soul had we received it. What we evaded would have been reality, had we understood it. We refused that for which we blindly and ignorantly longed; we denied that which we shall eternally need; we nodded, and hastily passed by Him whom we must find though we search forever in weariness and with hope deferred. Our souls, frightened, like ignorant virgins, have feared their fulfillment.

3

On Coming to Oneself

ALTHOUGH we dread the intimacy of religion, and seek in many ways to evade its disclosure of the soul, we cannot escape life, which often acts with a more ruthless violence in stripping us down until we face ourselves in all our naked need.

After the prodigal son had lost his resources, had fallen so far from Jewish honor as to tend swine, and had not even enough to eat, the scripture says "he came to himself." He had been stripped clean of everything, of his possessions, of his pride, and even of food—then he saw his actual self. It takes a great deal sometimes to reveal a man to himself. There are so many things that get between his eyes and his soul. It may be money, or his social standing, or an all too comfortable existence—none of them essentially evil, but nevertheless so obstructing a man's sight that he never glimpses himself behind them. The prodigal son, however, had these things violently torn away, leaving himself visible in all his need, and shame, and despair. Having come to himself, the scripture significantly continues, "He said, 'I will arise and go to my father.'"

It is not easy for any of us to get through all the coverings in which we are wrapped in order to find ourselves. There are so many things around us in which we are hidden, our image distorted, compromised, smothered, even obliterated. There are so many things we do in which we ourselves have no part, things done against our own will, things done out of necessity, things in which we put neither heart nor brain, jobs in which we have no interest, pastimes in which we have no delight, countless activities, stillborn and without the mark and life of our integrity upon them. Even at life's best, when we give ourselves completely to the work in hand, it is extraordinarily difficult to make the product of our labor, whatever it may be, communicate the spirit and the reality of the soul with which we made it. And whether our actions belie us or we never fully reveal ourselves in our action, it is hard indeed to get through the outer world of activities to the self which acted them.

Moreover, we have innumerable fences around us. They classify us by separating us. There is a racial fence, a national fence, a family fence. There is a fence of our trade or profession, another for our social class, one for our moral reputation, still another for our creed. And whenever we describe anyone, we use these fences more or less for the person himself—he is white, American, married or single, rich or poor, good or bad, banker or plumber, Catholic or Protestant. But after we have said all these things, we have only expressed what could be stated of countless others and we must ask the question again, "Who is he?" When the prodigal had come to himself, you will remember, he had lost all these fences—his wealth, his racial honor, his reputation and his standing—and there was really nothing left but the man himself, the human being, full of needs and crying hunger. Yet, if circumstances do not treat us rudely and sweep away these obstructions, we have the diffcult and baffling task of deliberately getting through these fences, wrappings and labels, if we are to come to ourselves.

I presume that we do not discover ourselves more often than we do, not because of the difficulty of getting through these baffling coverings, but rather because of the unpleasantness which we know awaits us at the center of our being. For whenever we have come to ourselves in moments of insight, when in the lightning flash of revelation we have seen what was in the darkness of our inner world, we have had a most uncomfortable experience. We are mixtures of good and evil, sometimes saint and sometimes sinner, with awful doubt and desperate faith wrestling forever in the deep abyss, and all the perennial paradoxes of death and God and love running like angry spears through the quiet heart, while the brain asks its innumerable questions, and the tongue babbles on with endless words, and the eyes busy themselves with many things, and the body is filled with its own anxieties!

Such a strange world do you and I enclose, a world of glory and shame, of tenderness and indifference, of wisdom and stupidity, of great things and mean, heroic and despicable at once. It is no wonder we flee from such contradiction, humiliation and embarrassment. No wonder, I say, we flee and find refuge in the calm orderliness of that halfway land between self and the world, not the self and not altogether the world, but the meeting place of the two in a man's work, in his reputation, in his activities, in his pleasures, and in his countless connections —a thousand little alleys down which we run to hide from what we carry in ourselves. This is why men do not like to think of themselves, why the modern world hates silence and solitude, why multitudes have left the Church, where in its essential function it is responsible for directing a man's attention to the nature of his life, its needs and limits, its unrealities and sins. This is why many churches have ceased to be churches, in order to please and entertain man rather than to glorify God. It is not that the fences keep us out, but that the tragic realities of our souls embarass us and humanly enough we flee to escape them.

In a memorable passage in *Wind, Sand*

and Stars Exupéry says, as he rides in an omnibus with government officials and clerks to the airfield:

Old bureaucrat, my comrade, it is not you who are to blame. No one ever helped you to escape. You, like a termite, built your peace by blocking up with cement every chink and cranny through which the light might pierce. You rolled yourself up into a ball in your genteel security, in routine, in the stifling conventions of provincial life, raising a modest rampart against the winds and the tides and the stars. You have chosen not to be perturbed by great problems, having trouble enough to forget your own fate as man. You are not the dweller upon an errant planet and do not ask yourself questions to which there are no answers. You are a petty bourgeois of Toulouse. Nobody grasped you by the shoulder while there was still time. Now the clay of which you were shaped has dried and hardened, and naught in you will ever awaken the sleeping musician, the poet, the astronomer that possibly inhabited you in the beginning.*

Indeed, how many ways we manage to lose man and to evade confronting our own nature. All the mad schemes of pleasure and excitement are escapes from the seriousness of life. The careening thoughtlessness, the precipitous lunging from one thing to another, the desire to be lifted by some intoxication, are all avenues away from man. And although we quickly recognise these as shallow diversions, we need to see just as plainly that the philosopher also manages to keep man out of his orderly jungle of profound abstractions, by which he explains everything but being human; that the scientist loses man in his placid copy of nature; that even the churchman may miss him by his casual respect for the Church and respectable society. Those men who seek to remind us of man are scarcely received with any warmth of welcome. Barth reminds us of our essential sin; Van Gogh paints the

---

* Antoine de Saint Exupéry, *Wind, Sand and Stars* (New York: Reynal & Hitchcock, 1939), p. 23.

agony of man's nature in the writing lines and flagrant colors of his canvases; Einstein includes the observer in the law, insisting upon the essential relativity of all the findings of science; and Heidegger recovers the tortured consciousness of man in his system of philosophy. But such men will not be popular, for we do not wish to be reminded of that which we strive so frantically to escape. In countless ways we surrender to the world and take refuge in its kaleidoscopic activies. We plunge into the ceaseless stream of events and live in a state of perpetual motion, where we may forget our own tragic mystery. By mutual relationships with a multitude of others as forgetful as ourselves we achieve in the mass a sense of solidness, permanence and self-sufficiency which belongs to none of us individually.

It is necessary, therefore, to ask plainly what it is from which we are running away. What are we under our contradictions, in back of our fences, within our unrevealed souls? We certainly do not flee from the body. It has its needs of food and clothing and shelter and companionship. For these things we work and enjoy working. Nor do we flee from the mind, for though it has its needs, we find answers for its questions, new fields for its curiosity and truth for its hunger, and we enjoy the search and the satisfaction. But deeper than physical care and intellectual perplexity, there is a realm of needs which these two do not touch. We are more than a body, though there are a few who maintain the doubtful honor of being satisfied with only that. We are also more than the brain, though there are some who see no advantage in pleading for more than that. We make no plea, but only say that a man may find a realm of need which neither brain nor body represents, and this realm is his self, his being human.

Here in this deep center, stripped of all pretensions and pride, of fences and labels and activities, we come upon a crossroads where everything under heaven meets, and in that meeting rises to self-consciousness. The universe here begins to know itself in all its grandeur and mystery, its beauty and brokenness. Here at this point the past and the future converge—here in man time falls away in two directions. Here the pain of its quick flight is felt like an arrow in his heart, and he knows its inevitable and irrevocable passage. He knows he was born into time and knows also he will die in time. All the past is gone—all the future lies subject to the question of his death. This one moment in which he is living is the only sure thing he has, and yet even this is about to be gone. All his past has been comprised of moments like this and whatever future he has will be the same, as temporary and as impermanent as this one which is passing away even as we speak of it. But there will come one moment which will be final, the very end of time, which we call death, and then there will be only one question that we can ask. Not what is his work, his race, his wealth, his poverty, his knowledge, his reputation, his prestige, but rather is he temporary like all the moments which made up his life, and which now are gone, or is he eternal? This is the question we flee, the embarrassment that drives us to hide in a hectic world of diversion and activity, the contradiction beneath all our other contradictions. This is our humanity, this is what I am—the question mark between the earth that is always passing away and a God who lives forever.

You see, if my body which I fed and sheltered and clothed and nurtured dies, and with it the brain and all the knowledge stored in its gray recesses and convolutions, what hope have I? Certainly none in the flesh, none in the brain, none in the world, none in time, therefore, I am hopeless. Stripped like the prodigal I come at last to know my poverty, my helplessness, my despair. "And when he came to himself, he said . . . 'I will arise and go to my father.'" Veritably this is my hope! All that I am seems temporary, a part of time, destined to end, but in the spirit of God, eternal and everlasting, there alone is my hope. So out of my desperate despair is born a desperate faith, the only kind of faith there is—the last cry of man stripped, and knowing his awful and infinite need.

You may ask, "Isn't it better not to think of myself, not to look for myself, not to ask these questions, to forget myself?" All I can say is that if you can live in this baffling world and never ask why you live; if you can breathe and watch your pulse beat, and dream and never ask unanswerable questions; if you see one die whom you love and never ask why he died and not you; if you can live knowing you too must die, though when you do not know, and never ask what then; if while you live you love and others love you, and you never wonder how it came about; if in life and love you think of this or that or the other thing, and never ask why you think or what your thinking or your loving or your living means—then I should say this truth has no meaning for you.

At least not now. It will never have meaning until you are awakened, shaken by some mysterious assault of God, penetrated by the sharp two-edged sword of love with its pain and death with its joy. But as long as you avoid yourself, you must realize that you also avoid God. For I am not speaking to you in behalf of mere selfish concern; I am directing you to discover that without which you will be a cipher taken over by the world's mock integers. Such mock integers Jesus recognized and declared for what they were worth. Wealth was one, which he plainly estimated as hostile to the spirit. But it was not merely on the basis of the shallow and rather sentimental notion that it deprived other men of possessions, but more essentially because an accumulation of possessions did two things. It supported a false security, and at the same time distracted the attention from man's essential being to the things he possessed. For the same reasons, he thought ill of power, and insisted that the first mark of greatness was its very opposite, humility. Moreover, he similarly suspected the nature of respectability, and chose for companions harlots and publicans in preference to Pharisees. In every one of these instances, wealth, power and man's own righteousness, Jesus saw the support of pride and the covering up of man's eternal mystery. They were mock integers and constituted no actual value in God's sight.

God and His favor are not to be found in the things the world can supply—wealth; nor in things man can do—power; nor in the reputation men earn by their external activities and appearances—respectability. God is to be reached back of all the fences, under all the contradictions, in the midst of the desperate despair, whenever a man is stripped clean and comes to himself. Then he also comes to God. Not because man and God are the same but because God is not to be reached by evading the starting point of one's own necessity and need.

Multitudes are saying, "But we do not need God. He is superfluous." If you are speaking of your body, you are quite right —your body will be satisfied with food and shelter and warmth and all this the world can supply. You are quite right if you mean that your brain does not need God. The world can be maintained, industry developed, machines invented—all without God or even the idea of God. But you—you who are temporary, you whose life is made of countless moments, all but one of which are gone forever, and this one even now is going, you who hang upon so slender a thread—how long can you get on without God? You who feel the mystery of time and the tragic anguish of man, through body and brain, you need God though body and brain may not. Without God you are nothing, a temporary moment, a twinge of pain in the endless night of being.

When the prodigal came to himself, he said, "I will arise and go to my father." When you and I come to ourselves, there is nowhere left to go but to the Father. I do not know how your fences will be shattered, or your labels burned, or your pride and pretension humbled—but I do know that the kingdom of God is still being taken by the desperate violence of men, who, having seen themselves, know their absolute and awful need of God.

4

Soul and Society

IF life can strip us down to the fundamental realities where God may be met, it must be said as honestly that the world in its ruthlessness may deprive a man, not only of extraneous encumbrances, but of his very soul. It may blur his spiritual identity and leave him utterly lost and bewildered. Plainly this world is not a fool's paradise where one may wander as one will without harm or hurt. There are hostile forces at work, and the common paths of man's life are beset with perils and temptations. What makes the danger grave is that the threat is subtle. The soul may be lost by such slow degrees and socially approved activities that it disappears before one is conscious of its going!

In the course of Western experience, what we mean by losing the soul has undergone various transformations. The picture uppermost in many minds today has been inherited from the imagery of the Middle Ages. It is a vision of damnation, vivid with the tortures of hell-fire, meted out by an angry and offended God. Imaginatively elaborated by the ecclesiastical painting of the medieval Church, it has been literally burned into our minds by Dante's classic epic, *The Divine Comedy*, and the more recent Protestant preachers of pioneer severity. For most moderns, however, the vision no longer seems a serious representation of reality.

Quite a different experience of lostness held sway at the end of the Roman Empire. It was not a matter of hell-fire and punishment, but the slow attrition of meaning and purpose in life which left people without any reason for living. Life simply became empty and unbearable. Increasing numbers of people felt that suicide was the only way out. Sleep was earth's best gift, and if perchance sleep were endless, then it was all the better. Those who went on living found little reason for it, and escaped the rigors of existence as best they could.

In many respects it would seem that our

age comes much closer to the Roman experience than it does to the medieval. People feel lost now not with the dramatic furor and everlasting flames of hell, but undramatically, senselessly, even dully. Our hell is literally desolate and hollow, haunted in turn by echoes and abrupt nightmares of universal violence and sadistic cruelty. This bland crisis, overlaid with the grinding enginery of war, the screaming headlines of the daily press, the chattering stupidities of radio and TV, the babel of crowds and the propaganda of states, tends to be hidden in the excitement and noise of our bedlamite civilization.

Yet cancer can be deadly in the busiest of bodies. Modern man carries the virus of this spiritual impotence within himself. Ibsen was already writing in the nineteenth century of Peer Gynt, the modern man, as one who was like an onion, all layers and no core. Dostoevski likewise described him as the "characterless man." Nietzsche dreaded this coming of the "Massenmensch." T. S. Eliot confessed our condition when he wrote his poem, "We are the hollow men, the men of straw." D. H. Lawrence portrayed us well when he suggested that we were like empty frames into which every passing fad stuck its head for a moment and then moved on to make room for the next one. The desolation of our inner life has surely signified the loss of our souls.

Each age has its own heresies and its peculiar hostilities to the life of the spirit. In ours the great tidal pressures are toward public-mindedness and mass opinion. The more outrageous forms of this life-drift have occurred in the Nazi regime in Germany, in the Fascist tyranny in Italy, and in the compulsive party-line in Russia. This virulent disease is not limited, however, by geographical or political boundaries. It has been stimulated on a wide scale by machine-dominated dynamics. So deeply marked have we been by the pattern of mass uniformity that we fear the slightest deviation from it at every level of our life. While we have boasted of our rugged individualism, we have toppled unknowingly into an attitude of mind and a frame of emotion which threatens to rob us of any substantial reality or spiritual identity.

This is what James Hilton has aptly characterized as "popular consent without private faith." In our time the private world has been taken over completely by public interests. Life itself has been externalized. We tend to have opinions about a thousand far-flung issues none of which mean anything at the heart of our being. This is the temptation by which the soul is painlessly deprived of all its proper life. What is left, a kind of soulless man, is whirled about so furiously by the world's frenzy and pummeled so brutally by its political violence, that he believes himself to be very much alive and really getting somewhere. If religion has any function to perform at this juncture of our destiny it is to save man from being swallowed up in the maw of such an anonymous public, which has taken to deifying itself in the state. The insane state is the ultimate consequence of the unreal individual.

Jung describes the nature of this problem when he says that "there is a vast outer realm and an equally vast inner realm; between these two stands Man, facing now one and now the other, and according to his mood or disposition, taking the one for absolute truth by denying or sacrificing the other." There is no fear that our age will be tempted to disregard the outer world. We have become its slaves, and in its present sickness its demands are undeniable. As for the inner world, any attention paid to it immediately calls forth opprobrious epithets of "morbid" or "introverted." Indeed, we fear to glance in the direction of that great inner world, where we should be at home but have long since departed and now have become as strangers and exiles.

Our most pressing task is to establish the reality of this private world. We must become acquainted with it, respect its hopes and fears, and learn how to handle its energies. William James said.

> The deepest thing in our nature is this dumb region of the heart in which we dwell along with our willingnesses and unwillingnesses, our faiths and our fears. Here is our deepest organ of communication with the nature of things; and compared with these concrete movements of our soul all

abstract statements and scientific arguments—the veto, for example, which the strict positivist pronounces upon our faith—sound to us like mere chatterings of the teeth.*

Whether such a discipline of restoring the soul can be accomplished without practicing withdrawal from the pressures of the modern world is highly doubtful. Some form of asceticism seems inescapable. The very minimum would seem to be the removal of our roots from the motives and satisfactions that now drive the world to its destructive manias. Until we withdraw, pull ourselves together, concentrate our purposes, and sharpen the discrimination by which we seek to "redeem the time" we will add only confusion to confusion. The foundation of private reality is the only hope of social solidarity.

It is this fact which we are beginning to glimpse in these revealing days. Community cannot be fashioned out of technological fabrications or political

* *The Will to Believe* (Longmans, Green & Co., 1912), p. 62.

coercions. The stuff that cements society together is secreted by the most intimate processes of man's life. Whenever the soul weakens, the community begins to disintegrate. The loss of one inevitably brings about the collapse of the other. This is spelled out in terms of war or some other violent expedient to compel a seeming order where there really is none.

The rediscovery of the true center of life in man waits upon his disillusionment with the mechanical juggernaut he has created. One of the unforgettable sentences in the striking story of *Kon-Tiki*, that voyage of six men on a straw and balsa raft, wafted 4,300 miles across the Pacific, is the following: "We realized after we had been on the way for some months that life had been full for men before the technical age; in fact, we discovered it was probably fuller and richer in many ways than the life of modern man."*

At this moment when man is beginning to sense the vacuity of his inner life religion stands to reaffirm its permanent

---

* Thor Heyerdahl in *Kon-Tiki* (Rand, McNally, 1950), p. 173.

and abiding significance. It refuses to compromise with the annihilation of man as such, and his transformation into a tool of the state. It demands recognition of his fundamental freedom as the only basis for social organization and the responsibility it entails. It will suffer in concentration camps and submit to death if need be, as it has in the past, but it will not turn its back on the private reality of the person.

Some religions may deny the reality of the outer world for the sake of enhancing the prestige of the inner, but Christianity has remained steadfastly realistic, denying neither the outer nor the inner. It holds the outer world in due reverence as the work of God and believes it to be the medium of His manifold benedictions. It holds the inner world to be marked peculiarly with sign of His intent. The soul has been granted the function of "naming" in the divine economy, that is, of bringing up to meaning all the things He created. As a soul, man is more than a created thing. He is not merely the recipient of environmental influence. He conditions the meaning of life; he determines the nature of reality; indeed, he redeems it by his spirit from its bondage to time.

Precisely on the basis that this inner reality is permanent and significant in the economy of life, religion posits its belief in immortality. This is not a matter of logic or argument. It is a conviction that something appears in the experience of man as he handles the circumstances of his life and the materials of the world, fashioning them to the glory he has dreamed, which is of a different order than the things with which he worked. In some such way we have come to feel that the soul is more than the stuff of which the earth is made, and bids fair to transcend the changes of mortal time.

This leads us very near the presence of God. As long as man seeks to escape from the actual substance of his own life, as modern custom tempts him to do, God can be nothing more than a distant dream, a childish remembrance, an ancient fear. This is in truth the modern counterpart of the story of the Prodigal Son who tried to live on the husks of a far country, only to find himself employed at tasks far below his proper station. It is only in the most intimate and immediate point of experience that God becomes a possibility. He is not to be found as a thing among other things. Not in a distant heaven beyond the stars nor in a well-fabricated system of ordered facts shall we ever find Him! He who made the stars and the worlds can only be found in the holiness of a profound privacy of being. It is at this point that we touch the nature of reality, and with it the very substance of eternity.

Out of such an experience we come to know what may be called the underived authority of the soul. It is the knowledge that by some mystery the deepest level of man is related to God and is inseparable from Him. This is the rock on which we may stand amid the tides and storms of our changing mortal life. Here we know that we are not dependent for our peace and joy upon the weather of the world, the pleasure of our fellows, or the prestige of our action. We will not need to be propped up by the praise of our friends nor will we be cast down by the attacks of our enemies.

It might seem, on the basis of this description, as if the soul were a hermit, content to turn its back on everything but its own concerns. But this is not so. Inevitably, once the soul has apprehended its own private reality, it will seek and enjoy true communion with the outer world in which it lives and by which its own existence is enriched. It will consider any relationship in life to be superficial or unreal which fails to reach this deep and abiding level where man himself is most real. Man may fulfill the demands of social existence, and be a respectable neighbor and a good citizen, but these things may be the sheerest kind of "worldliness," neither sustaining nor satisfying the fundamental desires of his eternal nature. It is only when he relates himself to others who have found life deep in the center where God is living and working that he will be able to share in a society explicitly practicing that freedom which can be achieved only in life with God. To those who do not know the abundance of such a fellowship, we can only say that we "belong to a church." The phrase itself will mean little to those who see it only through the narrow dimensions and futile associations of the world. Obviously it will not be a bond of perfection, for we who form it will to some degree distort it and deny it with our fallings away from our own deep center and from God. That is why it must be a fellowship of forgiveness. For although we and our fellows will often sin against it, there will be faith to forgive, knowing that we will find no peace or joy except in returning to the very center of life where God and man dwell together in gentleness and freedom.

It must be evident now why saving souls is more than a theological cliché. There is no way to hold society together, or to put it together when it has fallen apart, except by the establishment of a private world of reality in the people who constitute it. Without that core of essential integrity, the world becomes a chaos, at best a fabrication, hypocritically assuming the guise of vital order and falling willingly enough now and again into the passionate honesty of war.

The Church must stand at this uncomfortable juncture where souls, finding their own reality more or less, and disillusioned more or less with the inadequacies of the world, come together humbly and reverently to create a structure of communion out of the deepest and, at the same time, most precarious experiences of eternity. To lose our souls in such a time as this is tantamount to losing the world as well.

5

Loneliness and God

WHENEVER a human soul begins to be conscious of itself, the seed of loneliness is sown. Boys and girls, growing out of the thoughtless years into adulthood, enduring the awesome loneliness of mysterious experiences, tender and formless, filled with a strange splendor but fraught with frightening power, which no one else seems to see, or, seeing, to understand, are lonely. Mature men and women, initiated into all sorts of secrets and wisdom, gathering knowledge and accumulating understanding, seeking to share with one another the joy and the light which has come to them, but coming face to face in the very act of sharing with that which may not be shared, realizing what a disproportionate bulk of every truth and reality must remain unmoved behind the walls of the soul after language has done its utmost, they too are lonely!

They know that there are some things we cannot share—the incommunicable skill, the unteachable insight, the sincere affection, the experienced revelation. Older people treading each day in ranks that are constantly being thinned out, until what was once a solid phalanx of friends now moves across the long shadows of the sunset like lost stragglers seeking their company; older people not knowing one another or being so distant that their gestures are full of poignant hope and sadness mingled bravely together—here, too, is loneliness. Loneliness, tender and pleading for understanding in youth, frustrated and inevitable in maturity, mellowed and deepened with many memories in age—but always loneliness!

Somewhere deep within the center of this house of clay, always out of sight but never out of mind, we have an angel, tongueless and without speech, and we live our days, year after year, seeking some way by which that deep imprisoned self may communicate with other such angels in the many houses of clay who are our friends. With mystic symbols of language we fling out wordy messages across the windy gaps of the world, and what little we hear we piece together by help of the imagination so that it may make sense to us. Then after we have done all that we can with words, we learn the subtler ways of gesture, gestures of the eye and of the hand, of motion or no motion, through which the richer secrets of the self are spoken and understood, with quicker and more vivid comprehension. Yet with all that we can do, the more anxious we are to make known that which is essentially our own experience, the more certain we are doomed to disappointment. The words men utter may be the same, like cups all alike, but the meanings poured like wine into them are as various as the experiences of the men. And the more unique such experiences may be, the more certain they will be destined to the loneliness, not merely of willful misinterpretation, but of underestimation, of being identified with lesser or other things. We are lonely, alone in our house of clay.

When one sees John the Baptist and Jesus side by side, the contrast is interesting. John was a solitary, a voice in the wilderness, an ascetic deliberately choosing the way of solitude, but no word of loneliness ever breaks from his lips. Jesus, on the other hand, came not fasting but eating and drinking, congenial to the social occasions of the time, celebrating with his fellows the festive circumstances of the home and nation, but oh! how lonely! Lonely among the crowds, lonely in his own home with his mother and brothers and sisters, lonely among his own disciples.

Probably that loneliness can be reckoned best by the quick impulsiveness of his understanding of other lonely souls. Will there ever be such penetrating perception of its awfulness as when he rose to high defense of Mary, who, overwhelmed by the tragic sinfulness of herself, knowing her utter excommunication from the society of decent people, dared the further disgrace of Simon's house to pour the only thing she had left of any value upon the Master's feet? Or the mighty memory of him upon the Cross, who lifted up his head in the darkest loneliness of the world and shouted to the poor, bereft soul of the thief, "Today thou shalt be with me in paradise"? Two lonely men, cast off by the world, forgiving whatever had been between them, forgiving and forgetting the wrong that nailed them there, and finding in each other a hunger as necessary as their pain. Jesus lived among men, yet he was a lonely man, and he knew the loneliness of men.

It may seem a little strange that I should speak about loneliness to those who live in the crowded cities of our teeming world. In such a socialized world surely no one is lonely. Millions of us crowded compactly together, crowded into the vast hives of our apartments, crowded at work and crowded at play, with a million eyes relentlessly following us no matter where we go or what we do, with all our time devoured by the greedy maw of innumerable social relationships—what chance have we to be lonely! We are never, never alone!

Yet, never alone—we are lonely! Desperately lonely! For there is no loneliness like the loneliness of the crowd, like the loneliness of Jesus in the world that did not understand. It is one thing to choose deliberately the loneliness of the desert or the wilderness as did the monks of old. It is quite another thing to rush with a mighty hunger into the cities for companionship, to seek frantically for understanding, to fill days and nights and years with people, people, people, to pack ourselves so close together the grass cannot grow under our hurrying feet nor the winds blow anything but the dust of our ceaseless coming and going, to live not in ourselves but in everybody but ourselves, and then to have loneliness thrust like a knife between every man and his fellow, to have it fall like an acid upon our world until each man falls to the bottom alone! Here no man knows his neighbor, and at his death those who know him are too far to bid him farewell, and those who are near to let him down into his grave never saw his face. This is the loneliness of the city, aching with a void it tries to fill with desperate action, knowing its failure yet never admitting it. But why? Why should we be alone with so many near us?

Let us turn while this question hangs before our eyes to look upon the story of our lives. You and I, and all other men, are born into a family by the will of the flesh, determined out of mystery beyond our knowing, to be identified as the son or daughter of this man and this woman, to live this life with the name of this family upon us. This is the pattern we enter from the womb of darkness, this pattern and this name are our home, our all. Yet strangely enough we have scarcely begun to live before internal compulsions begin to push us out, to thrust us into the bewildering world of millions who make the world; a mysterious loneliness springs up amid the comfortable companionship of the family, an energetic loneliness empowered by unsatisfied desire for understanding sets us loose to look and choose among the world's like-natured for an answer that the family with all its close affection did not supply. To that end we leave our mother and father and cleave unto wife or husband.

But freeing ourselves from the family into which we were born by the will of the flesh, and in which we became aware of our loneliness, we turn and create a family in which the crosscurrents of profound loneliness and terrible intimacy must run and be enacted times without number and under innumerable designs. The angel in the deep of the clay still sighs in the dark night watches when there is silence to hear her. Day after day, entering the countless relationships of love and hate, of work and play, of desire and indifference, of service and sin, we are turned back baffled. Just as in the family into which we were plunged by birth, and in the family built around the most intimate understanding life vouchsafes to us, so in the many avenues of the world we come at last to see ourselves standing alone. With all sorts of men and women about us, using various means of communication, with the angel in the clay, there lies untouched and unmoved a level of life to which sooner or later we must give attention. The ultimate necessity, forced upon us by this social loneliness, is to know that we must be born, not only of the flesh, or of the will of man, or of the world, but of God. Put in its plainest terms it is this, that social relationships, however just and morally good, cannot take the place of spiritual relationship with God. The sum of all creatures will not assuage the hunger of man for the Creator. We may run out the tender fragile strands of human fellowship in a thousand directions but the resultant cobweb of mere gregariousness will not hide the yawning depths of that deeper hunger.

Whenever the awful loneliness of the angel in the clay beats with pain and anguish, man may frantically seek such satisfaction as his lust of gregariousness may afford, to drown in the city crowd, to melt into the mob mind, to gather affection at any price from any source. The terrible demand made by the love of God in the loneliness of his soul may be thwarted by the very kindliness and protection and comfort of his human fellowships. There is a call to be born of God, and that call is not to be answered by the thousand and one social amenities which may devour a man's time and energy. Terrible as it is, that loneliness, and the call it represents, is less terrible than the consequences to be faced when it is repudiated and existence shrinks to the frail thinness of mortal contacts which have neither depth nor height, neither heaven nor hell. This is our peril—that we may strive to satisfy our loneliness for God with the affection of men.

Let us know this, that the peril is

nowhere more real and continually possible of dire consequences than in the church. The reduction of divine worship to social fellowship, the substitution of familiarity of handshaking for the mystery of the spirit, may be abetted by the very quality of concern for our fellows which religion creates. But churches are never made out of the social cobwebs of men. The church is not my mother or my father, to whom I was born by the will of the flesh. Nor is it the innumerable social acquaintances to whom I am casually related by the will of the world in the necessities of work or play, for advantage or for pleasure. It is a group of people, each of whom is related to God, and because of that relationship, quite apart from any earthly tie, are related to one another. We are united not by business, not by a social class, not by moral conventions, not by race, not by tradition, not by education, but by the Spirit of God, unutterable but inescapable. That loneliness which this world, with all its clutter of human relationships, casual and intimate, cannot satisfy is the longing cry of man for God, the witness of a mighty

Father. Wherever two or three are gathered together, not for a pleasant time nor to fulfill their duties nor even to do good, but in the name of something beyond this human world, there is the making of a church, a little "colony of heaven."

6

The Singular Decision

IN loneliness we are separated from one another and from God, but we miss the spiritual meaning of this human burden when we fail to identify the responsibility it entails for each of us in the realm of decision.

In the most poignant of all Jesus' parables, that of Dives and Lazarus, there is told a story of a rich man and a poor man, and of their strange reversal of fortune.

Here is Lazarus, who all his life was held in contempt, who sought only to beg crumbs from a rich man's table, and whether he got them or not is a matter not spoken of in the parable; the dogs of the streets licked his sores and he was an object of considerable pity. And yet, it was this man, so pitied and disdained in life, who in Abraham's bosom knows a blessedness that the man of prestige and influence never gets. The full poignance of this comes only when we hear Father Abraham saying to the rich man who had been accustomed to considerable prestige and self-satisfaction, respectability and feeling that he really had his place in the world, "My son, there is a gulf fixed, so that even if Larazus would like to put a drop of water on the tip of your tongue, he cannot."

Well, there is a gulf fixed in human life —now, here, everywhere, and always. You will not wait until you arrive either in torment or in bliss to see that gulf and to know that it is rigidly established. When David had news brought to him of his son Absalom's death, he knew Absalom had revolted and rebelled against him and had done everything a son could do that would have brought pain and anguish to his father's heart. He had been the kind of boy that no father would want, yet when the news came, you remember the cry that was wrenched out of David's heart, "O my son, my son Absalom! Would I had died for thee!" Even between father and son a gulf had been fixed and though David would like to have done certain things for

Absalom and given him certain ideas or ideals or principles or motives, he could not. At one time or another every one of us would like to have done something for someone we loved; and yet, though love is a bond as clear and as strong as any in the world, there are some things that cannot be carried across the bridge. The gulf is fixed.

It is this, essentially, that makes all the difference in the world between what we in our modern day have called propaganda and what the Church and the Bible have always called the grace of God, glad news, evangelism. For propaganda is something that can be spread across the earth, great blankets of it, radio blankets, newspaper blankets, magazine blankets, pamphlet blankets. You can drop it out of airplanes; you can shoot it through microphones; you can thunder it into the ears of a people; you can put it into pictures and symbols until at last you can have every man, woman and child in the country crying, "Heil Hitler." You can have them all braying in the same tone at the same time and believing that they are worshipping truth. This is propaganda. It is now the method of mass communication, utilized by mass production in a mass culture for mass consumption. It is now the operation of governmental and national influence in satellite and buffer states conducted by Soviet Russia and the United States of America and any nation that must maintain its place in the world. It will create common behavior; it will make what the Germans call *Gleichschaltung*, similarity, people wearing the same clothes, thinking the same thoughts, feeling that they belong to the same kind of people until at last everybody has the feeling that he is strong because he is part of something big and no one would do anything to create a rift in it.

But over against this, there is another truth that can never be poured into the airways. It can never be put into the newspapers. It can never be spread across the face of the earth in magazines and pictures. It is, in a sense, a truth that is ineffable. It is a truth that does not come by the amplified voice. It is a truth that comes from God to man's soul, and it does not come from outside of man's soul into it. It comes from within man's soul where

God touches the most intimate center of his life. It does not come when a man proceeds outwardly toward stars, or nature, or the universe. It occurs when a man comes to himself where only he lives and no one with him. No other soul touches that deep center. There, at that point, where he is utterly alone, at the point where he must die—for men die alone—there is God. Words may come from Him, up from within, and then this truth is a different truth from the truth created by propaganda.

This is the truth of evangelism, of the glad news, of the gospel of Jesus. There is a gulf fixed between you and me, between you and everybody else; there is a gulf fixed between you and your relatives, between a man and his wife, between a father and his sons, so that Jesus said if you do not hate your father and mother, if you do not hate your children, "you cannot follow me." All this hate is, is a recognition that we are standing absolutely alone at a place where we must accept God or refuse Him. We cannot accept Him on the basis of our family's accepting Him; we cannot refuse Him because nobody else in the neighborhood acknowledges Him. We must accept or refuse Him on the basis that we are taking this responsibility ourselves, and that henceforth we belong to Him or we do not belong to Him.

Now we might like to give God to our father or to our son or to our wife, but we cannot. We can pray to God that He will work His wonders to perform and come into their lives; we may live our lives so that there may shine through them some semblance of the fact that we have found God and God has found us; but there is no propaganda, there are no set words, there are no methods by which one can insinuate God into another person's life. God comes into that life as He came into ours, by mysterious, inward, intimate, individual experience.

How much we would like to substitute for that hard doctrine, doctrinal uniformity! How pleasant that is in our day! How many churches are trying to build a firmer structure of doctrinal uniformity, so that everybody believes the same things, in the same way! How many churches would be delighted to have a kind of moral uniformity so that all people would act alike and their consciences would all behave the same way. They would all believe that respectability was the same kind of thing! How much we would like to have denominational uniformity! In fact, that is why we have denominations. As church members, we do not like differences; we do not like it that God acts differently with different people and so we get all the people together who have a similar experience and we try to elevate and exalt that uniformity into a church.

When I say, "I believe," I am not talking merely about ideas or words or doctrines. The words "I believe" are just as deeply personal as the words "I love." John's gospel is very theological, but it is the very gospel in which it is declared that love is of God and all who love are of God. To say that I believe in God means also that I love God. And this belief is as intense and as passionate and as deep growing as love. Ask a man and a woman who say they love each other what they mean and it is essentially ineffable. When they say they believe in each other, they are saying the same thing. And so when we say "I love God," or "I believe in God," we do not set up a creed. This is to say that somewhere in the very center of life there is a relationship to God at once of believing and of loving Him.

Walt Whitman once said, "Music is what awakens in a person when the instruments remind him." Religion is what comes to life in us when we read the Bible with understanding and insight. What is conversion but the occasion in life when a man or a woman suddenly turns from the thousand and one distractions of the outer world to that deepest center of human life which we call the soul. This is where he or she is absolutely alone and comes face to face with the source of life and the meaning of it. At this point all life is in revolution and falls into a new perspective. What is prayer but the continual returning to that center where we come face to face with the mystery of our relationship to God.

"My son, there is a gulf fixed," and no man can possibly come back to help you even though he would like to. You are carrying within your soul the burden of that freedom which God gave you when

He created you. Freedom merely means this: that nobody under heaven can ever help you decide what you must decide for yourself. It means that you must make the decision and you can never put the blame on anybody else. "Oh, but, Father Abraham," Dives says, "do send Lazarus back across the line of death and let him talk to my brothers—I have five of them." You can hear in his voice the love he bears them—"so that they will never come to this place of torment." And then Father Abraham says this strange thing, "They have Moses and the Prophets and if they do not hear them they would give no hospitality to a man though he was raised from the dead."

Now some may feel that this is a discouraging concept. But it is so only because we have grown accustomed to the idea that all we have to do is to congregate in great masses, in front of loudspeakers or vast printing presses and be immersed in the tide of truth, until all men know it. God's truth is not known that way, but it is just as available as any other truth and only requires a man's individual attention and responsibility to be accepted. In fact,

God is more available to men than the daily newspaper or the radio if they are only willing to pay attention to their own existence.

Moreover, there is significance in the remark that Galileo made when he was accused of moving God too far out of the universe so that men grew discouraged and felt forsaken. "The sun," he said, "which has all those planets revolving about it and dependent on it for their orderly functions can ripen a bunch of grapes as if it had nothing else in the world to do." God is able to tend your soul as if He had nothing else in the world to do.

This is the glad news—that you can never evade your freedom by becoming a part of the anonymous crowd, but God always keeps you as though you were the only partner He had in the universe. And if you say No, it is your sin and nobody else's, and if you say Yes, it is your bliss that you may share with many.

7

The Eternal and Its Substitutes

THUS far we have considered the soul largely in terms of its own reality, its fears, its loneliness, its decision. Now we seek to follow it into the world where it will transform things into high meanings, revealing their true glory, or be reduced to a thing itself.

From a half-forgotten page of reading, an old custom of the Puritan settlers suggests itself as a parable of our situation. Each day they went down to the edge of the sea and looked into its vastness, thinking the long, long thoughts of those who had traveled into a far country for the making of a new world. But as time went on, the sea was taken for granted, and the settlers were more and more preoccupied with the immediate concerns of their busy lives. Then there grew up along the edge of the sea warehouses, piers and walls, until even if they had wanted to see it, it would not have been easily visible. The greatness of that illimitable expanse, the far horizon, had vanished from their experience, and they were the smaller for its disappearance.

Something like this has been happening in our own day at a much profounder level. While we have been exploring the dark reaches of interstellar space and revealing our universe to be bigger than anything the ancients ever dreamed about, we have been losing or willfully discarding something like the vastness of the sea. The early Christians lived in the presence of God, in a world where He did things, and the waves of His mercy and wrath touched their hearts and ran along the shores of all their thoughts. For them, heaven and hell were very close realities. They were conscious of eternity as a sea that surrounded them, and they thought much on their own death and immortality. They were in the midst of an infinite scenery, most of which has vanished from our sight, the warehouses and the preoccupations of this frenzied world having hidden it from us.

One can see something of the way in

which we have been stripped of this larger world of eternal things by comparing the art of the Middle Ages, with our own. Some time ago there appeared in *Life* a reproduction of a painting of the Battle of Lepanto in which the little navies were shown in combat in the harbor, and the skies above them filled with heavenly hosts of patron saints and angels, with even the Mother of God engaged in sanguine battle, assisting their favorites below. You will remember, without difficulty, innumerable paintings of that era when not only the hosts of heaven but of hell as well were pictured within the same perspective of this mortal earth. In the greatest book of the Middle Ages, *The Divine Comedy*, Dante includes within its vision the dimensions of heaven, hell and purgatory. In our modern paintings the angels, devils and saints, future wrath or reward, have all vanished. It is a smaller canvas, a much more naturalistic one in which the artist puts down only what can be seen with the eyes of flesh. Somehow or other, this too is like a parable wherein we see how much we have lost of that eternal sea which once laved the shores of our dreaming, daring souls.

It is not strange that the eternal has grown to be a word full of vagueness and uncertainty. If we ever knew what it meant, we have forgotten; if our parents or fore-fathers were friends with it, we have either not been introduced or have moved away from it. When we come near it, we are a bit uncomfortable and frightened. We touch it and run. We cannot seem to find a place where we can stand and look into its vastness. We are fascinated by it and yet we frantically try to escape it. Still, this life without the eternal is hopeless. History is little more than a madhouse, and faith itself has neither root nor substance. Eternity is the actual ground out of which all our religious notions and experiences grow.

With the loss of eternity as the basic ground of our religious life, our natural hunger for it has sought for some kind of substitute. We have put false infinites in the place of the eternal. We crowd the canvas with hysterical activity, excitement and emotion, painting it all in bizarre colors, and distorting life in such a way that it attracts attention. We try to make up for the loss of the eternal by filling our days and nights with more events, adding one thing to another as fast as possible, in the hope of giving substance to what seems so thin. We are very much like one of John Dos Passos' characters who wants to ride on every train, go to every town and city, work at every job, live in every boarding house, sleep in every bed and read every book. Nothing less than devouring the world will satisfy him. Obviously, the eternal is not found merely by adding things together. The eternal may come to you in one thing, but if you dwell on the surface of a thousand things you only avoid it.

Sören Kierkegaard passionately satirizes such a way of life:

> Of all ridiculous things the most ridiculous seems to me, to be busy—to be a man who is brisk about his food and his work. Therefore, whenever I see a fly settling, in the decisive moment, on the nose of such a person of affairs; or if he is spattered with mud from a carriage which drives past him in still greater

haste; or the drawbridge opens up before; or a tile falls down and knocks him dead, then I laugh heartily. And who indeed could help laughing? What, I wonder, do these busy folks get done? Are they not to be classed with the woman who in her confusion about the house being on fire carried out the fire-tongs? What things of greater account, do you suppose, will they rescue from life's great conflagration?*

Americans are particularly subject to this heresy because of their tremendous energy and overweening desire to go everywhere and see everything.

Another false infinite is our worship of bigness. Pliny the Elder once said of the Romans that when they failed to make anything beautiful, they made it big. It is as if being unable to find the eternal within life, we try to build something like Babel, the ultimate in size, that reaches heaven and earth and time behind it. Thus we build the biggest bridge, the greatest city,

---

* "Selections from the Writings of Sören Kierkegaard," University of Texas *Bulletin* No. 2326, 1932.

the tallest building, only to realize that none of these things uncover the humbler glory of the eternal.

Probably a subtler form of the same heresy is to spread something out until it becomes universal, finding a peculiar satisfaction in world-wide organizations whether they are commercial, political or religious. The false infinite of a superficial collectivity is just as bad as the false infinite of devouring the world of events. Truth is no truer in the aggregate of humanity than it is in the heart of one person. The eternal is not created or achieved by universal agreement.

But we may also deal in a positive way with the eternal. We will find the eternal in at least three essential experiences. In its most elementary form it will concern our consciousness of mystery. How far that has dwindled in recent years can be estimated by the vogue of photographic literature of all sorts. Cameralike realism has overwhelmed modern writing. Sinclair Lewis and others, along with the picture magazines, have eliminated the sense of the mysterious and substituted in its place the curious, the natural, and the banal.

A few years ago Kenneth Grahame wrote a book called *Wind in the Willows*, full of a mystery in which life became substantial and sustaining in character, and when he was asked why he had written almost entirely for children, he replied:

The most priceless possession of the human race is the wonder of the world. Yet latterly, the utmost endeavors of mankind have been directed toward the dissipation of that wonder . . . . Children are not merely people; they are the only really living people that have been left to us in an over-weary world. Any normal child will instinctively agree with your own American poet, Walt Whitman, when he said, "To me, every hour of the day and night is an unspeakable perfect miracle."★

There is a little chance of recovering the

★ Clayton Hamilton, as quoted in the Introduction by Elspeth Grahame to *First Whisper of "The Wind in the Willows"* (London: Methuen & Co. Ltd., 1944), p. 27.

sense of reality in the worship of God unless there is some living capacity for wonder and awe in the hearts of those who come to church. Without this, worship will be degraded by attempts to make it interesting, novel, even fantastic. Until we can see in the life we live, in the commonplace circumstances that fill our nights and days, in the bodies we wear and the brains by which we think, something of that vast sea of mystery in which all things move and live and have their being, we shall not know how to bend the knee in prayer or how to sing the praise of God in spirit and in truth. To deal with eternity is, at its most elementary level, to be conscious of an impressive and uninterrupted world of wonder.

The second aspect of dealing with eternity concerns man's own death. This is the threat that hangs like a Damoclean sword over every moment of his pilgrimage. It is not alone that somewhere in the future there is the inevitable necessity of dying, but that this shadow is cast across all the days of his life. In everything he does there is the implicit question as to whether or not this will be of any meaning or significance in that final judgment. It is thus that man's life is deepened by a dignity and consecrated by an awesome knowledge of its own end. If this subjects him only to worry and fear, then his whole life is a kind of death; but if he is "joined to the eternal" as Augustine says, if in the midst of this life's decay and passing away he has been able to lay up for himself treasures in heaven, experiences of an invulnerable sort, then his life is not death, but life indeed, life eternal. Dealing with the eternal at this second level means to find peace in the midst of all the changes of time, because there is an unchanging kingdom in which our hearts are always at home.

The eternal never appears quite the same. What was seen in the Parthenon will reappear in the Cathedral at Rheims, and that will be born again in the Taj Mahal or in the Lincoln Memorial. The grandeur that was in Bach finds a different voice in Beethoven, and is reborn in Brahms. Until we can identify the unchanging under the garments of time, the eternal in the son of man, we will be wandering pilgrims without a home. Something of the truth of this is evident in the way Thomas Mann tells the Joseph story, so that we live in the experience, not of one who died many thousands of years ago, but rather of one so like ourselves that what he knew and suffered becomes the very story of our inner selves. This is the abrogation of time, the meaning of the myth, the sustaining strength of religious rites. It is where time and eternity fulfill their purpose in each other.

The third aspect of dealing with eternity concerns the purpose for which God created men. Paul called it the redemption of the world; our time prefers the word "creativeness." It is our task to reveal the world's undisclosed resources and possibilities, much as we have taken the stubborn materials of earth and fashioned them into a violin, and with it given further expression to the dreams of beauty haunting our lives. The world is spiritualized in man. It finds its freedom and its eternity in him. In his soul it is redeemed from the bondage of mere repetition, illuminated by new and vaster purposes, and enhanced by the gift of his vision and manifold self. Even at the most modest estimate, it is man who gives meaning to the world, creating with it much that would remain sticks and stones without him.

It is in this area that we are able to discern the kind of actions which are appropriate to dealing with the eternal. It is here that faith, forgiveness, peace, freedom and humility all rise into true meaning, and can be understood and practiced as part of an intelligible system of life. There is no affirmative way to deal with the imperfections of his life except by faith; no way to keep freedom among the souls of men except by forgiveness; no way to be humble unless man finds somewhere in the structure of his world the transcending glory of the eternal before which he bends his knee in wonder and in praise. These are all the fruits of dealing with eternity and are not to be known in any other way. They become utterly irrelevant in a grossly utilitarian or naturalistic world.

In older days it was said of a certain one that he was a "godly man." We are not accustomed to use the phrase any more, or certainly not as freely as once it was used, but there is something in the phrase that points to one who made himself known to his fellows as a man who dealt with eternal things. He may not have been very rich or very prudent in the ways of the world; he may not have been honored for his achievements or widely known for his name in the newspaper, but the world in which he lived knew that it had within its life one whose vision and wisdom transcended its petty limits, who took the measure of this world, fearlessly and tenderly, standing always humbly and calmly before the vast sea of its mystery

8

Spiritual Health

THE body has a health of its own, and we are usually quick to discern by pain and discomfort when it is offended. The mind, too, has its own health, but because it is much more subtle than that of the body, we are not as quick to detect the aberrations which in time may develop into serious mental illness. Now the soul, vague as it seems, nevertheless has a health of its own, obviously much more subtle than that of the mind or the body, so that we are not as conscious of the sins against it or the deviations that indicate its lack of balance.

One cannot deny that body and mind are sustained and kept in proper operation by sensible attention to their needs and appropriate activities. Strangely enough, one might think by the way people live that the spirit, which is much more elusive and at the precarious edge of man's evolving consciousness, could be expected to survive the grossest neglect, as if it were something that could be wrapped up, put away and ignored, and then claimed at some future date when it would be needed!

To be whole, or healthy, or holy, all come to about the same thing. One of the things which is disconcerting to many people reading the New Testament is the way in which sins and sickness are assumed to be related. In psychosomatic medicine today, however, we are discovering that health is a matter which concerns the mind and soul as well as the body. Fundamentally, Christianity has been engaged in persuading people to be entire or whole, to fulfill all their human capacities in the most adequate way. Its practices of worship and communion, of prayer and humility and forgiveness, are not additions to a good life, but the means by which a good life is perfected in a vigorous and abundant health of spiritual activity.

The first characteristic of spiritual health is indicated in the natural world by the relationship of systole and diastole, the principle of expansion and contraction.

The heart beating and resting, the lungs inhaling and exhaling, the body sleeping and waking, the seasons of winter and summer—everywhere a dialectic of opposites in which wholeness and health are manifested. It would be a strange thing if this were not equally true of the soul's life.

When either side of this dialectic breaks down, man is subject to dissolution or death. If he sleeps all the time, or if he cannot sleep at all, then obviously he is not well. So in the spiritual realm, if he does not reckon with the systole and diastole of the soul, he is liable to the derangement of energy that ends finally in nothing less than spiritual insanity of one sort of another.

Certainly nothing is more obvious in the present condition of man's spirit than his lack of peace, or contentment, or deep and rich renewal of his life. Modern man seems unable to shut the door on the world, to enter his own closet, to pray in secret, to find an inner quietness, to restore his soul by resting back upon the life from which he came as he restores his physical strength by sleep. Although Moses entered the mountain, Jeremiah the potter's house, Jesus the wilderness, we in our time fear to waste time by such action. We are cursed in a sense with spiritual insomnia. Even when we pray, we are so verbal-minded, that we think we cannot commune with God except we busy ourselves with much speaking.

Probably nothing so accurately marks our lack of spiritual renewal as our failure to listen; to listen profoundly and intently to life and what it has to say. We are verbose, noisily, incessantly verbose. The air is jammed, packed with rivers of radio words tumbling over each other and filling our days and nights with an endless rigamarole. Our newpapers are gigantic collections of words, with new editions appearing before we have had a chance to read even the old headlines. We are a garrulous, word-fevered, tongue-crazy race.

Recently I sat with a prominent educator. He talked brilliantly; he asked questions and answered them before anyone could reply, and if they did reply he did not hear it. He rushed, mentally out of breath, from subject to subject. He was an important man, doing many things and doing them well, but he had lost the power of listening to anything or anybody outside his own personal machinery. If a man gets where he does not know how to listen to another man, to listen for what is in the other man, I have grave doubts as to whether he can possibly listen to God. After all, the fundamental requirement of prayer is to be able to listen. One of the most arresting sentences in Werner Jaeger's study of Greek civilization is the one in which he says:

> Periclean Athens, mistress of a mighty empire, was flooded with influences of many different kinds and origins, and despite her brilliant expertness in every sphere of art and practical life, she was about to lose her spiritual foothold. Intoxicated by the exuberance of her own verbosity, she had in the briefest of moments talked all traditional values out of existence.*

* Werner Jaeger, *Paideia*, tr, by Gilbert Highet (New York: Oxford, 1939), Vol. II, p. 28.

Surely for us in Western civilization, so extremely energetic and practical that we tend to ignore the necessity of spiritual renewal, as if one could do without rest or sleep, there is a critical danger that we may exhaust ourselves by failing to pay attention to the sustaining sources of our inner lives. How much we do is thin and shadowy; how much of our life has grown journalistically shallow, like our very newspapers. To listen is actually the affirmative action of our spiritual capacity making itself felt in life. It is a sign of spiritual health and vitality. As the poet Rilke said:

> Hear, O my heart, as only
> Saints have heard; heard till the giant call
> Lifted them off the ground; yet they went impossibly
> On with their kneeling, in undistracted attention;
> So inherently hearers. Not that you could endure
> The voice of God—far from it! But hark to the suspiration

The uninterrupted news that grows
   out of silence!*

It is not enough to fling our wordy prayers upward. We have a fundamental need to thrust our roots downward, deeply penetrating our own existence, pondering the intimate inwardness of life, seeking to keep touch with the vast and wordless sea of being beneath us, from whence our strength and power comes, and by which we are sustained by intimations and vital urgencies. The health of our soul is in the systole and diastole of its own dialectic; if it is to work, it must rest; if it is to speak, it must listen. How great a skill it is to listen, so that in the quiet peace of the soul there can be heard the word of truth spoken for the first time, or the voice of the Eternal, that still, small voice, which is never heralded with trumpets or the mighty clamor of the mob!

In the second place, the health of the soul may be seen in its understanding use

---

* R. M. Rilke, *Duino Elegies*, translated by J. B. Leishman and Stephen Spender (New York: W. W. Norton, 1939), p. 23. Used by permission.

of appropriate means for its expression and fulfillment. To use the wrong tools for any job botches the result. Because we are living in an age of exceptional scientific popularity, we have been tempted to use the instruments and means so successful in the laboratory in the field of the spirit. Thus we have tried to sustain the spirit with abstractions, literal creeds, formulas and exact definitions. This pervasive literalness is a blight of death to the soul, and produces only fanaticism and a dubious pharisaical zeal.

The appropriate means of communication and thus of communion for the spirit are not primarily verbal. They are symbols, rites and stories. These are not to be interpreted literally. We of the Protestant faith are peculiarly poverty stricken, our souls barren of this rich and needful material. Our forefathers, sensing the idolatry and superstition of the Romish practices of their day, swept out all the symbols in one ruthless cleansing of the temple; equally in revolt against the pomp of kings and courts, the rites were also eliminated; and with the coming of the historical passion of the nineteenth century, the great stories of the Bible were subjected to a scrutiny that discovered certain doubts of their historicity, so they they too were flung to the winds. Thus we stand bereft of a language native and appropriate for the soul.

The symbols, rites and stories will always be discarded if they are to be judged from literal standards. They are obviously not literal truths. But from spiritual standards, from the viewpoint of the soul itself, its requirements, its expression, its means of communication, these discards rise into magnificent meaning. They are the signs of experiences so basic and eternal to the life of human beings that they never fit perfectly into any one histoical event, but they are the essence and truth of all existence as human beings know life on its spiritual level. Symbol is the most flexible of all language, and speaks to a level of heart and mind that words never reach. Rites are repeatable actions in which life's deepest glories are remembered and the soul reminded of its benediction in these things. The stories of Eden, the Tower of Babel, the parables and the life of Christ all have truths that evade the literal nets of the historically wise. They are the ageless formulary in concrete terms of unending human experience. In all of them the eternal and the historical meet and fulfill each other in such perfection that the truth is neither abstract nor merely local. It becomes rooted in life, but not limited by time or space. To be on the outside of such things, to be unable to use them, is indeed to be poor in spiritual health, for in them are the ample means of expression and communion for the soul.

In the third place, the healthy soul manifests its strength by a simplification of life, without falling on the one hand into abstraction or on the other into idolatry. The former is a deceptive escape from the rough and tumble existence of this concrete, everyday world with its confusion and embarrassment, and the unrelenting necessity to identify the evidences of God's grace in it. The latter is equally a deception and an unreality, for it anchors God superstitiously at some one spot in time or history and denies Him the freedom of eternity. Never to put your finger down to affirm God's presence in this place is to live forever outside of His kingdom; to put it down and never move it is to mistake a souvenir for God. A healthy soul is bold enough to affirm God in the midst of temporal imperfections, and strong enough to follow Him in the pilgrimage of moving time.

In our time one of the signs of spiritual imbalance is in our inflated pretensions and anxieties. We take the whole world on our shoulders as if we were God, or at least as if there were no God. We work ourselves into a frenzy about things too far away for us to solve, or impertinently think that our generation will solve all the miseries men have borne since the beginning of time.

Nowhere in all history is spiritual simplification more magnificently revealed than in Christ himself. He does not dominate the world by stretching himself over it in publicity or propaganda. He lives in a corner of no great repute; he meets the needs of men and women and little children caught in the tangle of hate and shame; he talks with no kings, seeks no throne, has no authority or prestige. He is meek, a lowly man, of no reputation, numbered with transgressors, accepting the shame of his death. Yet what he did was done so perfectly, so truthfully fulfilling everything that man has dreamed man ought to be, so fully revealing what seemed to be the only kind of God we could intelligently, hopefully worship that in him we have said that the Word—that eternal wisdom of God—became carnate, a living person. To simplify life is to treat it with such reverence, in every common casual ordinary event and person, that it will be transformed as a sacrament in which God's grace is revealed and by which we find together the communion of an endless peace and joy.

In the fourth place, the human soul is not whole or healthy unless it has found God. Without Him it is isolated, cut off, groundless and restless. Man's nature is incurably metaphysical; his peace is not to be found in animal placidity. If he renounces his soul, he drops below the brute world, as we tragically know from the horrible Nazi experiment. If he renounces God, as Russia does, he makes his politics a religion. He must make some guess as to the meaning of life and the purpose of history. He probes beyond things seen for answers to questions he alone asks. He wants truth; he is willing to die for beauty; he subjects himself to trying disciplines to be good. Man at his healthiest is a worshiper, a kneeling man, listening intently and desperately to life that he might reply in such a sacramental way, such an adequate response, that what he has heard may be fulfilled in and through him. This is the very will of God waiting to be done on earth as it is in heaven.

9

Hiding Places of Power

WITH what refreshment come those words from Isaiah:

Hast thou not known? hast thou not heard, that the ever-lasting God, the Lord, the Creator of the ends of the earth, fainteth not, neither is weary? there is no searching of his understanding. He giveth power to the faint; and to them that have no might he increaseth strength. Even the youths shall faint and be weary, and the young men shall utterly fall: But they that wait upon the Lord shall renew their strength; they shall mount up with wings as eagles; they shall run, and not be weary; and they shall walk, and not faint.

When one comes into the New Testament, this sense of power continues. Paul said:

> For I am not ashamed of the gospel of Christ: for it is the power of God. . . .
>
> I can do all things through Christ which strengtheneth me. . . .
>
> I know both how to be abased, and I know how to abound. . . .
>
> I am persuaded, that neither death, nor life, nor angels, nor principalities, nor powers, nor things present, nor things to come, nor height, nor depth, nor any other creature, shall be able to separate us from the love of God, which is in Christ Jesus our Lord.

In our day, we have been somewhat overwhelmed by the discovery of power which resides in the atom. By technical and scientific penetration, we have been able to go down into this deep invisible well and unlock this storehouse of almost inestimable amounts of energy. So far we have only used it for the annihilation of human beings. Whether we shall be able to find some other use for it still remains to be seen. But we are in the presence of something so fundamental and essential, so gigantic and tremendous, that for the first time in our generation men have grown afraid and have had the experience of awe.

Now there is in human life a like reservoir of power. Sometimes it is available to our use and other times it seems locked up and barricaded behind peculiar formations of hesitancy and caution and fear. One can see periods of history as in the New Testament when it seems as if some people found a key that unlocked this deep reservoir and then they swept across the earth with powers and a freedom from fear and a spontaneity that they had not known for hundreds of years. There are other periods when mankind is dormant, when it is as if a dark cloud had rolled in and all the elements of man's spirit had gone to sleep and there was no spontaneity, no ongoing delight, no faith that brought new visions to man's aspiring mind. All things lay as if they were dead. What makes the difference?

All of us know that there are experiences when, in a moment of crisis as when a house is burning, people will pick up trunks and large, heavy objects and carry them to safety, and then afterward are totally unable to lift them. Where does the power come from? Some of us know that when the pressure is on us and there is a necessity for it, we can work night and day, seemingly tireless, and then, at other moments, the most routine sort of existence tires us completely. Where does this power come from? We know some people who are endlessly active with minds and hearts fruitful to the utmost, and others with energies and powers equal in every way, who are handicapped, harnessed and padlocked. What they have within them they cannot use.

Why is it that Jesus announced his gospel in the terms, "I bring glad news; I bring news of liberation for those who are in prison, for those who are suffering shame, for those who are fearful, for those who are blind." It was not that he was going to unlock jails. It was that people like you and me, whose lives are somehow caught between that fullest expression of the power God vested in us and a kind of just ordinary, everyday, get-along-as-best-we-can sort of existence, might be unlocked, set free, to act in the boldness and fullness of that power which was ours by reason of God's creation.

One of the things that locks up this power in any man is fear or doubt or despair. If a man doubts too much he will be paralyzed. If a man doubts too much, he will be cautious. If a man despairs he will not care to do anything. Guilt also locks up a man; not only the guilt he feels but the guilt that he forgets which long ago turned the key. So multitudes of people go through life having forgotten the time and the incident when the key was turned, but unable to do one tenth of what they ought to do under God's grace.

Triviality and shallowness! The world's triumph is nowhere more evident than when it is able to get men and women to make their relationships with one another trivial and superficial. No greater evil can come into the Christian fellowship than to lose its first high glory of the love of God, and that vision of the soul's journey in the mind of God, to come down and diddle-daddle with a thousand picayune things that have no meaning or place in His kingdom. This too robs men of power. Sören Kierkegaard felt this pettiness keenly and compares it with what he sees in the New Testament.

> Oh, but when I read the New Testament I get the impression that in God's opinion every man is a giant. . . . There is nothing which every one is so much afraid of as getting to know how prodigiously much he is capable of. Thou art capable—wouldst thou know of what thou art capable? Of living in poverty! Thou art capable of enduring almost every possible ill treatment. . . . How ironical that every man is designed to be an Atlas, capable of bearing the weight of the world—and then to see what men we are; and alas, how sorry a thing it is that we ourselves are to blame for what we are!*

The first thing that can unlock power is forgiveness. The Christian gospel is absolutely right; it is psychologically true when it says to the world, "The thing you need more than anything else is forgiveness. We

---

* Walter Lowrie, *Sören Kierkegaard* (New York: Oxford, 1936), p. 540.

can promise you this stupendous gift of the forgiveness of God. We have a record which men have kept from the earliest times called the Bible in which this forgiveness is portrayed over and over and over in a thousand manifold experiences of people living in different times and undergoing different experiences."

There is nothing in the world as valuable as forgiveness. It unlocks the store house of power and gives freedom to people shackled in ancient chains of fear and guilt and shame and disgrace. I suspect that one of the reasons why the psychiatrists are so busy and are so popular in the modern world is that the church has long since forgotten that its main business is not to judge but to forgive. People are finding forgiveness in the hands of a psychiatrist when often in the hands of the church they find only harsh, moralistic, pharisaical criticism by a group of people bent on respectability and conformity to it. No church has sinned so badly in this respect as the Protestant church.

Péguy, writing some of the finest and most spiritually cognizant poetry of our time, is daring enough to put some words into the mouth of God. He thinks of God as looking down upon the earth, seeing man prepare to go to bed. The man has said his prayers and climbed into bed to rest and (if I may paraphrase Péguy*) God says, "Man is a funny creature. Just look at him now. He has said his prayers, he has asked forgiveness; and I've already forgiven him; yet he is plaguing his heart out over sins he committed today when he ought to relax and go sleep; there is nothing on earth quite as good as sleep. I have given it to man so that he might rest and be strengthened for the morrow; my forgiveness is in his sleep. Why can't he give up a little bit and let me take care of him? Why must he plague himself all night long about these things when he ought to put them in my hands and let me take care of them?" Forgiveness unlocks the tight heart and says, "God, help me," in the faith that God will help, knows how to help, and that sleep is the very sign and symbol of His forgiveness, of the resto-

---

* Charles Péguy, *Basic Verities* (New York: Pantheon, 1943), p. 217.

ration of our soul, as well as the reinvigoration of our body.

It is because forgiveness is the thing which first unlocks power that we turn secondly to what we have always called faith. What do we mean by faith? Do we mean that we have certain doctrines in which we believe? Certainly, but that is a secondary matter. The first thing we mean by faith is that there is help available to us over which we have no essential control. We do not possess the solution of all our problems. We know that we have sinned, but we also know that God will help us even in our sin, will lift us and restore us. This faith is confident, it knows that if we open our hearts, if we get to sleep, if we relax, if we are quiet, grace will come.

Out of one of the historical events which determined the character of Jewish faith comes the story of Moses' dialogue with God. When Moses requests God's name that he might identify Him to the people, God replies, "I am that I am." This is indeed cryptic, but it is illuminated by Martin Buber's interpretation that God was actually saying, "I shall be there as there I shall be." Obviously this meant that God could not be identified once and for all in the manifold diversity of mortal circumstance, but would be found in each occasion as He revealed Himself in it. His grace will be available for us everywhere, any time. It was on this foundation stone that the faith of the ancient Israelites was built and on which, at last, that moving glory of the grace of Jesus was manifested to men so that he could say to sinners, "Look at your experience; look at what you have been through. Do you not see that in these things God was working to perform miracles and wonders? If you once recognize God's presence, you will assist Him and not work against Him."

Faith is not an intellectual thing. It has its intellectual aftermath but fundamentally it is a deep-hearted, single-minded, full-bodied confidence that in the world there are forces and powers, principalities and graces waiting to come in, to make more adequate our own life and more abundant our own living of it. The poet calls it inspiration; the historian calls it perspective; the scientist calls it understanding; but everywhere in the world there is grace waiting to do more for us than we have been able to do for ourselves. This is faith which knows that when I step out there will be strength given to do things that I would not know how to do by myself. Have you ever tried to operate involuntary muscles by a volitional effort? Everything we do, we do by the strength of God or we would get nothing done.

Now the third thing is, that once we have turned the key with forgivenesss and have entered into the confidence that there are forces and powers waiting to help us, we enter a fellowship with others who are trying to live lives that are open on all sides, inviting the grace of God and seeking it. This experience is a recognition that one of the sources of power is in a communion where we release and support one another's strength. We cannot live independent, isolated lives as much as we in America think we can. We have overestimated our individual strength and particularly among intellectual and educated people this overestimation has wrought great damage, so that they are no longer supported and sustained by a living comradeship, but each man turns distorted, twisted, in his own peculiar idiosyncrasy.

How much this world desires such fellowship can only be guessed by the desperate and pathetic substitutes it is willing to accept. T. S. Eliot's theatrical symbol of *The Cocktail Party* raises the issue unforgettably of people bereft of any substantial relationship and finding their very existence empty, tasteless, banal. These people are shadows, hungering and thirsting in a dry and weary land, where conversation has turned into chitchat and a cheap and temporary communion is bought with a cocktail or two. In this world that has fallen so far apart, leaving no center at all, the cocktail party is the last desperate secular device substituted for the grace of Holy Communion. To find our power released in the full freedom of faith in one another, liberated by our generous forgiveness of one another, at the highest and deepest level of our being is incomparably more realistic than the detour of alcoholic relaxation. But if this fellowship that worships God in repentance and joy, turns from forgiveness and faith, down to an orgy of minor matters until we grow as trivial and as superficially-minded as the world, then woe unto us, for the glory has departed and the power of God's grace has been betrayed.

The fourth key to unlock power is humility. Now with humility I am not referring to some kind of craven slavishness that says, "Well, I'm not as good as you are, of course." This is an outrageous hypocrisy. It has no place in Christianity. Christian humility is not craven; Christian humility is hunger for something vaster, larger, deeper, and higher than anything we have known. Humility is recognizing that my life is not self-dependent, self-created but that all I do comes from God and the mystery of God. Humility is earnestness and hunger and striving and desire. It is the opposite of complacency and indifference and cravenness. Humility is prayer. I do not mean the prayers that one writes or speaks, but rather in the larger sense when one bows his life and waits and says, "This is not enough; there must be something deeper and better that I have not achieved"; or when one looks at what he has done and says, "This isn't as good as I wanted it to be." Prayer of this kind takes all that a man is and has been and lifts his whole life up, beyond, and out toward a glory that might yet be—this is prayer and this is humility! After all humility is merely knowing that there is a kingdom of God more glorious than anything man has yet known. He has had a taste of it; he has seen a bit of it; he has understood it here and there, but he is humbled and humiliated by the little he himself has been able to possess of it.

These are keys to power—forgiveness, confidence in the grace of God, a fellowship of communion with common aims and purposes, and humility which comes whenever a man has met the glory of God. Unless somewhere one of these keys can be turned, the kingdom of glory will not come and we will never know what it is to live in the fullness of life with that God who giveth power to the faint.

10

The Realm of Peace

IT is little wonder that the ancient Jews after they had been conquered, sent into exile, scattered across the face of the earth, suffering all sorts of indignities, as well as catastrophe, had grown distraught of soul, insecure of mind and heart, and yearned for some kind of deep abiding peace. Nevertheless in our time, though we have not suffered the same catastrophes in this country and certainly have not been scattered by the conquest of a foreign power, we too have known something of tragedy so deeply unsettling that we also have had yearnings for peace. Not for the peace of the sort that politicians make, or that treaties establish, but of the profounder sort that gives satisfaction and confidence and contentment to the human soul.

Yet there has been something in our life that has destroyed the chance of that kind of peace. Almost all of us were originally, so to speak, emigrants, cast out of Europe by violent situations, thrust into a new land which demanded violent resolutions of life's problems, and who with tremendous energy and initiative conquered frontier after frontier and laid a whole continent at our disposal, until at last we exhausted the more obvious horizons. But we still have within ourselves this overweening energy, this extraordinary habit of aggressiveness, this wish to conquer and to dominate. And so in this restless, ruthless, changing, scattering, tormented and tormenting population there are the very seeds and sources of our unrest while we want deeply to find peace, a peace we destroy almost at the moment of wanting.

Quite apart from this, it would still remain true that as we live from day to day in our personal and individual lives we have grown somewhat tired of the incessant activity. A good part of it we cannot find any reasonable purpose for doing, yet for some strange reason seem to be enslaved by it so that we can no longer discontinue it even though we think it would be better for us if we were not caught in it. We are rushed from house to work and from work to house, from occasion to occasion, from circumstance to circumstance, from committee to committee, from one organization to another, until there is no rest, and without rest, can there be peace? Without a feeling of deep establishment in something so abiding and so fertile that our motives and our satisfactions are realized it it, we will be cursed in skimming the surface all the time, or in leaving one thing undone to pick up something else that in turn will never get done. If somehow we could get out of this fatiguing and frustrating and futile situation it might be that peace could come back to our unquiet souls!

There is a phrase of a poet that recurs to me again and again like a refrain, "Call back the heart to quietness." But how call it back to quietness in a world as restless, as insecure, as cursed with the wish to do many things in the hope that by getting them all done the world will be saved from disaster? How call it back from this kind of noisy anguish when there seems to be nothing in us that will give us purpose and direction, integrity and reality, deep enough to satisfy us? This is one of our most grievous problems today.

There really are two worlds. There is a world where the only things that get done are those which a man puts his hand to and turns a wheel until at last the product is made. This is the world in which most of us live most of the time. It is a world which calls for energy expended, for ambition to succeed, for initiative to be exerted. It is a world in which almost all the peoples of the world are now deeply involved in the belief in action. Then there is another world. When we look at the stars there is no action which we can take that will make any difference. They *are*, they exist, they persist. We cannot manipulate them, we cannot shift them, we cannot even use them. They are beyond the hands and the purposes and the greed and the restless ambition of men. So there are many things like the stars beyond this utilitarian greed, this restless anxiety, this guilty ambition, this aggressiveness that tries to dominate and control and utilize everything in the world. There are many things which do not lend themselves to this kind of overt action but will only come to man when he is willing to consider the heavens, so to speak, and with his own hands folded and his own soul quiet he is willing to receive. He puts his heart at the service of something; he does not seek to impose his demands upon it.

Now this second world is the world of faith, the world of art, the world of religion, the world of prayer, the world of the spirit. It is the world of inspiration, the world of peace, the world of plenty, the world of the Infinite and the Eternal. But this second world does not seem very practical; we cannot use it, we cannot value it in dollars and cents; we cannot work it into the economic and industrial system very well; we cannot make it seem practicable in terms of getting things done.

But for all that, this other world is the world out of which this world first came, and by which it gets all its meanings, its joys, and its peace, and by which this world is finally judged. And if this world be not a servant of that other world, this world will disintegrate into chaos, and from chaos into destruction and desolation. And that which seemed so practical, so utilitarian, so absolutely firm and permanent and obvious, will at last be cast to the winds.

Read the book of Revelation and note how this man, who had seen the city of God, turns to Rome—so mighty, so practical, so tremendous in its military might, so wonderful in its economic arrangements, so perfect in its engineering skill, so technically proficient in arranging the life of men—and declares that it will fall, be broken rock upon rock, while the great captains will stand by and lament, "What city is like unto this city?"

We have loved America; we have loved this Western civilization with its science and invention, magnificent products of the power of man to impose his will and to use the energies of the world. But all this will be as nothing and will be swept into desert dust if somehow it does not receive its implicating powers and peace and joy out of this other world where there are stars that cannot be handled and a God who cannot be bent to man's will.

We see often enough that religion is just one more escape from reality by which men turn their backs upon the hard facts of this world. But there is another kind of escape in this modern world by which men turn their backs upon that other realm from which this world gains its meaning, its purpose, and its final validity. And the escapists who live always in this world of practical affairs and think that they are realists, I have no doubt whatsoever, will come to the day when all the practical powers which they hold in their hands will be as destructive as the powers which Rome held and they will see these flaunted permanences of government, of technical proficiencies, and of industrial productivity, all vanish away as if they did not exist. No, there are two kinds of escapists. There are those who do not live at all in a practical world, and they seek some ivory tower away from it; but let us not be mistaken—there are other escapists who are living entirely in the market place and putting upon life only the value of its economic and industrial efficiency. And these people are more grossly escapists than the visionary.

There is in this other world a peace. The difference, one has said, between one who has been converted and one who has not been, is that the man who has been converted has lost the strain from his life—the anguish of restlessness, the torment of anxiety, the devil at one's heels driving a man like a slave to do more and more, out of which he gains and is satisfied less and less. In religion there ought to be peace, so abiding and so deep and so satisfying that this world of ordinary practicality in which violences and catastrophes occur will no longer have power to overwhelm us. This is the peace that passes understanding, so that a Christian can be thrown into jail and persecuted, sent into the arena and lose his life, and yet in all these things remain at a deep level undisturbed by it. This was what amazed the brave practical Roman.

Where does this peace come from? Why is it that in Jesus with all his strength there is an abiding gentleness? There is no strain, there is no tremendous energy of guilt, there is peace. When he sits down to talk with a man he talks with him as if this was eternal. When he stands at the well curb at Sychar he talks with the woman from the village as if this was all that had to be done in this world. Why does he say to his disciples, "Are there not twelve hours in a day? Don't fret yourselves the way the Gentiles do. They try to lord it over one another, to dominate one another and to get better jobs and positions, to be a little higher in the community and to satisfy themselves with the success of their ambition, but you shall be children, dependent children of God, who, if you seek his kingdom, will give you all the things you need." Where does this peace come from that was in Jesus' life, that took the strain out of it and left him not like a rushing cataract but like a quiet pool, clear, still, deep, cool, refreshing?

First of all it can be seen that this peace came from the resources of God. In that world there is an eternal, everlasting and infinite peace. There is a stupendous richness beyond all that we can dream or think. In this world there are things and each one is limited. There are people and we are mortal. So that in this limited world, this finite, mortal world, we are always grabbing, clutching, gathering, possessing, accumulating, in the hope that we will overcome its piecemeal character. But in that world of religion we do not have to grab or clutch, or seek or possess, or accumulate; the treasures of heaven are given to us while we sleep, while we do nothing, for it is our Father's good will to give us this kingdom which was founded at the creation of the world. This is the free grace of salvation, this is the gratuitousness of God's love. This is His mercy, a gift from one who is so infinitely capable that to our limited selves there are no limits to what He can do for us. One may have peace in the religious realm and not have it overwhelmed by the catastrophes of life because it is endless, infinite. One can never have it in the world of practicality where there are inevitable changes and catastrophes and limitations and death and decay. All man's grabbing and gathering will at last find him with full barns and an empty soul. Then comes the disillusionment, the mask shall be taken from the empty face—there is no sign of life beyond the eye.

Now this gift is more than just the gift of plenty. It is the gift of forgiveness. Nothing keeps us running so madly from one thing to another as our guilt. We did not do the last thing very well so now we will try to do this a little better. And this does not get done either, so we drive ourselves from thing to thing, never accomplishing quite what we wanted to, and accumulating guilt all the while beneath us and in back of us that presses us still on and on with increasing terror and haunting power. God says, "Forget it, I have forgiven you; let it go, be quiet, be still and know that I am God. With all your fretful anxieties you cannot bring the kingdom of God. I have made it; I have brought it into being; I have created it; and here is it in men's hearts waiting. You did not put it there and you did not make it by your actions. All that you can do is to see it and to love it and to affirm it and accept it. It is yours for nothing; you are forgiven. I have made the sun to rise on the good and on the evil and you are evil as well as good. I have made the rain to fall on the just and on the unjust." And this magnificence of mercy of which there is no limit, comes upon us to give us freedom, the freedom of faith in God, that God does care for us and that in His providence there is a peace that the world can neither give nor take away.

Those who crowd themselves in vast groups in which there is no communion will be lonely and restless. The man who is alone with God, however, the man who has considered the heavens and has lived in the realm where he does not make but receives a grace for which he is thankful, this man's soul is vast with meaning, deep with strength, anchored in the eternal and abiding in its peace, although he dwells in the midst of the desert. There is no anxiety, worry, and restless rushing to get somewhere, away from where he is to a place in which he is no better satisfied. Peace is not easy to accomplish in our day but it is impossible to find it or to enjoy it outside that other world that supervenes on this one through which God's grace pours as plentifully as the rays of the sun and refreshingly as the fall of the rain. Rilke, with poetic unmistakableness, suggests the truth in a phrase:

> With his left hand God governs the creation, The right merely reposes on his knee.

---

* R. M. Rilke, *Later Poems*, translated by J. B. Leishman (London: Hogarth Press, 1938), p. 130. Used by permission.

11

Dealing with Spiritual Slackness

THE Psalmist said that he had gone to church; he had praised God with great rejoicing; he had kept the holy days with devotion and sacrifice, and yet for all these things his soul was cast down within him and he was puzzled and not a little ashamed. I presume that we too often must confess to ourselves if to no one else that even though we had gone to church and raised our voices in song and offered our prayer in the uttermost of devotion, yet somehow or other our soul was cast down within us and we were troubled why it should be so and not a little ashamed, or else we might have been willing to confess it more often. For the truth of the matter is that keeping the holy days, attending the worship in the sanctuary and offering prayers do not in any wise guarantee that a man shall be without these dark experiences which overwhelm the soul and leave him as if forsaken of God.

The Psalms are full of it from beginning to end; the 63rd Psalm says, "My soul thirsteth for thee [O God], in a dry and weary land, where no water is." The 88th Psalm cries out, "Thou hast laid me in the lowest depths, even in the deepest darkness and I am shut up and I cannot come out." Job struggles with it and says, "Why didst thou ever take me from the womb? Why could I not have died there in the dark?" (Moffatt). Bunyan, the Baptist, knew it; Fox, the Quaker, knew it; John of the Cross, the Catholic, knew it; men of every age, of every clime, of every sect have suffered under it.

You remember when the rich young ruler asked, "What shall I do to inherit eternal life?" Jesus asked him what his habit of life had been, and one can almost hear the tone of despair with which he says, "I have kept the whole law from my youth up." This was what had bothered the young man, not his wealth. He had gone to church; he had kept the law; he had worked hard being good; and yet he had no feeling that there was an eternal life within this. He was spiritually slack; he lived in a dry, weary land where there was no water; his soul was cast down within him.

In the Middle Ages, there were seven well recognized sins, seven deadly sins. One could wish we could recognize as many now. One of those seven deadly sins was known as "accidie." There is no word in our tongue for it. It was spiritual torpor. It was aridity, dryness, sterility, weariness; a kind of numbness that crept across the soul. Why should this be? Why should you and I, week after week and year after year, attend the services of the church; why should we pray day after day and year after year; why should we in a thousand different ways seek to live just as goodly lives as we can and then find all this amounted to a spirit of heaviness? Nothing comes out of it and our inner lives feel dead and heavy.

There are some things that can be said about it. First of all this is not an exceptional thing, peculiar to you as an individual. It is not because you have not tried. It will come to those most of all who have tried and who are the most honest about themselves. When we begin to play as if every service of worship were a glorious adventure of the spirit we are not being truthful. This thing does not happen to mortal men and if it were going to happen it would happen to the geniuses of the race like Schweitzer or Martin Luther or Fox or John of the Cross or Theresa of Avila or the Psalmist or Jeremiah or Isaiah. The truth of it is that every one of these freely and frankly confessed that this thing overwhelmed him time and time again and made it seem as though God had never visited him, as though the word had never burned upon his tongue and as though his experience had been a dream, a vacant, empty, futile dream. No, this belongs to us as one of the crosses of our human experience and it will pass more quickly if we will admit it and recognize it, rather than be deceitful about it and make a pleasant pose of always enjoying what obviously we do not enjoy.

The second thing is that some of this may come out of just sheer fatigue. There is nothing truer of our modern world than that we are overwhelmed with too many stimuli. We do not have merely our own family, our own friends, our own neighborhood on our minds. We have multiplied this by a tremendous manifold through the radio, the newspaper, moving picture, and television. We are forcing upon our poor mortal selves a burden of emotion that we have not earned or have not deserved concerning things about which we can do nothing because they are at the ends of the earth.

Once we have exhausted ourselves with these things we are slack when it comes to experiencing something that does concern us. The sheer fatigue of a dog who could smell and sniff all the bones of the world would represent very well the condition we are in. We are stimulated beyond our capacity and are tired, tired with wanting, tired with despair, tired with sympathy, tired with trying. It is not surprising that after going through this ordeal we come on Sundays with sheer fatigue to try to lift our voices to the level of praise and to exalt our hearts to the place of worship. Is it any wonder that usually we do not succeed?

Moreover, I suspect that just because we have this habit of being overwhelmed with too many stimuli we try to protect ourselves, and so we withhold our heart and soul from a great many things in the world, until naturally enough it gets to be a habit and we withhold ourselves from everything just a little bit. We save ourselves a little bit all along the line and then this habit of withholding ourselves means we go through everything that happens only partly in it, sometimes not at all in it but just going through the motions of it and therefore we get nothing out of it. Sunday worship can be attended without being shared. Sharing is costly. It takes imagination; it takes emotion; it takes an effort to take down the bars, but we withhold ourselves and are poverty-stricken. Nothing comes because nothing is given.

And last of all, it could be that we just grow too sure. We have been through this service a thousand times, a million times. We have prayed and prayed and prayed and know what to expect and what not to expect. We have sung our psalms and expect nothing new in them. We have lived our lives and the ruts are plain and the paths are all marked and we never go into a new one. We are absolutely secure and certain, and the end of absolute security is utter complacency and out of this there is nothing but death, darkness, routine, sterility, a dry and weary land where one motion follows another and no thought need ever be given to it. To be sure is to lose life.

What can be said about a positive way of handling this? After we have dealt with all the negative ways in which we might have come to this experience, we must confess that being human we do all come to it and experience it most plainly even at the time when we wish we were not experiencing it. We come into worship and we want to worship, but we are dead. We want to praise God, but there is a spirit of heaviness over us. We want to exalt our souls but they are cast down within us. What shall we do?

First, we must get back to the center of things. Dislocate life from all the peripheral concerns, from the thousand and one activities, and return to the center where life is a very humble miracle and mystery, back to the place where we cannot fold our hands without clasping a strange, inexplicable experience of being and of existence.

Get back to the center where God is at the very point of that abyss of need at which we stand. Get back to the center for this is the only place from whence life comes to the spirit. There is no life outside of God. All things are dark, dry and weary, heavy and deathly. This is why the wages of sin is death. Life is in God and only in God.

Perhaps I can hear you saying, "But that is the one thing we cannot find. Everything is dark. God is the very thing we have difficulty in discovering when worship slackens and our souls are cast down." Yes, you are right. I must go back to what Jesus advised the young man to do after he said, "I have done all these things from my youth up": "Sell all thou hast." I presume that most of us have been intent upon this tremendous command to sell everything and get rid of all one's possessions. But I have a feeling that there was something deeper even than that, as radical as that may seem, namely, that Jesus was trying to tell this man, "Make a totally new start. Get rid of everything on which you have been leaning and start all over again. Get to the center of your very life and even without God start to follow these humble paths of anguish and lean on nothing, nothing at all. Make a new beginning. You have done it this way, you have done it that way; you have followed this custom, that practice. Break them. No matter how good those things are, break them and start again and refresh yourself and dig a new well somewhere."

Someone said of Renoir that he never painted one day as he did the day before. There is something here for the Christian to remember. One ought never to do exactly the same thing the same way as it was done before. If it is done too often it will deaden. God is infinite and therefore is to be approached in infinitely different ways. One ought not to limit one's own experience of God to one experience. Start over again. Start humbly. Make a new beginning. It is said that Beethoven discarded thirteen different attempts before he finally captured the unmistakeable glory he wanted for the funeral march in his Eroica Symphony. Christian experience is forever in need of beginning again. To keep the finger on one spot too long makes an idol of it and blinds us to the revelation of God elsewhere. Every experience in time and space has its limits, and to forget that is to turn away from life and its eternal liveliness. Make new beginnings! God's world is infinite and can well afford all the beginnings we dare to make.

Finally we can reach out for help. We are not living in an impoverished world, even though we have come to a place of barren rock and sand in our individual pilgrimage. In this wilderness the everlasting arms are beneath us. The kingdom of God still exists, and there is grace for a new beginning. We can reach out to souls stronger than ourselves and redeem our days. We can reach out to Moses and stand with him before the burning bush that was not consumed, and kneeling share the glory of that hour. We can walk down into the potter's house with Jeremiah and watch the molding of the clay, while the prophet broods on the mysteries of God working with His people. We can listen to the voice of that troubadour of God, good St. Francis, singing with such gay faith that all the ages have been inspired by it. The Bible and the history of the Church are full of such resources waiting to restore our souls to their proper brightness and strength. Such infinite hospitalities of the spirit are an everlasting refuge for the soul cast down and weary in the exhaustion of its own limited powers.

Rabindranath Tagore once said:

> I thought that my voyage had come to its end at the last limit of my power—that the path before me was closed, that provisions were exhausted and the time come to take shelter in a silent obscurity.
>
> But I find that thy will knows no end in me. And when old words die out on the tongue, new melodies break forth from the heart; and when the old tracks are lost, new country is revealed with its wonders.

One of the texts in the New Testament which we have reserved for use at funerals only but which I think ought to be claimed for life first of all is the one in which John

---

* *Gitanjali*, 37. From *Collected Poems and Plays of Rabindranath Tagore* (New York: The Macmillan Co., 1937), p. 17. Used by permission.

hears the voice from heaven saying, "Behold, I make all things new. Write: for these words are faithful and true." You will know a thousand deaths before you die. Your soul will grow slack and weary and will lie down and die. It will be as if it was buried, many times. And then, out of newness of life you shall find a resurrection and in that resurrection all things shall be made new and you will enter into a larger abundance than ever before. But it will only be if you have a strength to confess you have died and want to be resurrected and will enter through travail into a greater glory and a wider abundance and a deeper eternity. "We must find some place," said Yeats, "upon the Tree of Life for the Phoenix nest." *Why art thou cast down within me, O my soul? . . . We must be born again. . . . Behold, I will make all things new.*

12

Prayer and Life

WHEN we are born into this world, it is not long before we are introduced to the pleasure and problem of communicating with people. There is something in the human individual that would like to say itself and receive an answer from beings like itself. Very early in our infancy we begin to utilize all manner of things as symbols, gestures, actions which would communicate to others some of the impulses and the wants within our own selves.

After a time we begin to use language, falteringly, clumsily, but nevertheless language in which the wants and impulses and hopes and aspirations that are within are clarified and communicated, answered and responded to, and thereby enriched by the people who live around us. It is true that we have to find out how to use the words we inherit and to some degree we make them over to fit ourselves. All the while, underneath our language there is something inside ourselves that wants to say itself and receive from the outside some answer, and thus to be enhanced and possibly glorified in an experience that could not be known in the isolated confinement of one individual. The character of our own experience, what we have known and suffered, what we have seen and heard, what we have thought and divined, all this, or the lack of it, enters into our words and language so that it is true that the character of the soul may be known by the conversation it keeps.

Moreover, as we learn to talk with one another, we grow to understand that there is something more to language than the mere talking of it. The most talkative people are not always the wisest, and they are not always the most communicative. One of the difficulties which we face in our own time is that we have multiplied words to the impoverishment of wisdom. We are a newspaper-ridden, magazine monopolized generation, verbose, as William James put it, with verbalities.

Now if this is true of us on the human

level, there is something in us also that wants to say itself, but that wants an answer not from another man but from God. We are born, not only by the will of the flesh, which puts us in our place in the race; not only according to the will of the world, which puts us in our place in the social environment and in human intercourse; but we are also born with the stamp of eternity on us. We call that eternity the soul and the soul wants to say itself and to get an answer from its natural Companion and Creator, God Himself.

In our day we are suffering from severe disconnection. Our communications are broken. I suppose that is one of the reasons why most of us rush into vast cities where we can be very close together, with the hope that being close together we may be reconnected in a vital relationship with the things from which we have been disconnected. We have become disconnected from nature. Here cities and science and educational sophistication have helped to broaden the gap. Moreover, we are separate from one another by the kind of individualism that we have inherited, so that when we come together to sit in a group where we might have an experience both mutual and common, we find ourselves so thoroughly boarded up with cautions and reserves that we cannot do more than meet at the outer edges, rather than at the vital center. The changes that have been so rapid and have introduced us so abruptly to a technological and atomic age have separated us from the past, and we are no longer part of a tradition.

Back of and prior to all these disconnections is the fact that for a long time Western civilization has been separated from God. In short, we are living in a disconnected age and this makes prayer extremely difficult. It makes it hard because imaginatively we cannot jump the gap between our finite selves and the Infinite, and deeper still have lost the skill and wisdom to handle things by wholes rather than by their parts.

Our disconnectedness has made it difficult for us to pray. Yet we are born into the flesh and into a world where we are inescapably caught in infinite ramifications so complete that many observers say that we are ever-lastingly doing only what we have been forced to do by our environment and our inheritance. There is an iron tissue of law that surrounds us and we are held inevitably in its grip. There is truth to this, so much truth that each one of us, by each act and deed, even by each thought and impulse, registers our will upon the whole life of the entire universe. The smallest thing we do at last has ramifications that affect ultimately the end of all things. Just as dropping the smallest pebble in the sea does in some infinitesimal way affect the tides and waves at the farthest continent's end, so what you and I do in the secrecy of our hearts at last affects the ultimate whole of all.

Now prayer is the acceptance of this condition of our life. It accepts this infinite series of ramifications and it tries to develop a kind of sensitiveness and imagination that will consecrate the individual's relationship to the ultimate end of life and the purpose that is in all things. Prayer is trying to remain connected with the entire environment, not only the nearest part of it. Prayer is trying to admit and confess that we are tied to God inevitably because we are part of the world which God made and if we revolt from the world, think that it is of no meaning, count it as making no sense at all, and say, "I will have nothing to do with it"; yet even then we are still related to the whole of things and the end of everything by our warfare against it.

Prayer is the assumption that we are related to God and the ultimate end of His purposes and creation. Prayer takes up this vast burden, lifting it with all its imaginative insight, and puts the self into the entire picture of life, grappling with all those forces that would at last adjust the relationship so finely, so willingly, that what is being done helps everywhere rather than injures. The adjustment having been made, one will speak the language of the eternal and the infinite, and learning to speak it, will get an answer.

I suspect that the reason so many prayers are a frustration is that not only do we use the language of earth, which we have inherited and which we cannot avoid, but we have never employed it in the service of heaven. That is to say, our prayers have been earthly prayers for earthly ends, without being consecrated to this higher purpose of the adjustment and the surrender of the self to the eternal and infinite, the very purpose of Almighty God. Prayer is the whole self saying itself to the whole mystery of life and holding conversation. Just as in our human intercourse talkativeness does not mean communication, so in prayer the more words we use and the oftener we pray have no connection with the vitality and validity of what we do. Sometimes the best prayer has no words. Certainly prayer is not a sudden flinging of oneself into the presence of God with a veritable storm of words and then, without waiting for an answer, an equally abrupt rushing out of His presence, even before the words have ceased to sound.

No, the words of a prayer depend for their meaning on the silences of prayer, and if there are no silences we can well be sure that there is no meaning to the words. What is a conversation but the peculiar balance between keeping quiet and speaking? A strange thing that continues to grow apace with our talkative prayers is that we assume that it is left to us to find God. Spiritually speaking, one discovers sooner or later that God is usually much more capable of finding us than we are of finding God. Prayer in itself is the answer to God's searching. When we have lifted up our voice, it is because God has already been at work in our life.

Indeed, this is what the Church has always meant when it talked about the "prevenience" of God; namely that God is always in an experience before you come to it, and when you come to it, He, being already there, is willing to bless you. Bernard of Clairvaux says:

> Do you awake? Well, God is also awake. If you rise in the night time, if you anticipate to your utmost your earliest awaking, you will find Him waking— you will never anticipate His own awakeness. In such an intercourse you will always be rash if you attribute any priority and predominant share to yourself; for He loves both more than you, and before you love at all.*

When you offer a prayer you offer it with God's grace, you offer it with God's

---

* Quoted by Douglas Steere in *Prayer and Worship* (Haddam, Conn.: Hazen Books, 1938), p. 10.

strength, you offer it because you have already been found of God.

Why should this not be true? You are held in the hands of these infinite ramifications and you cannot do anything that does not affect the ultimate end of all things and the whole of things, and if this be true, then it is also true that He who is the Lord of all this, who is in it and made it and seeks to develop it, shall not leave one single element in it without His care and concern. Dr. Bowne used to say that of all creation the most responsive must be God. The *most* responsive must be God. Is that not our own characterization of human worth: the better the man, the more responsive he is? Then God must be so far greater in His responsiveness than anyone we have ever known that the comparison falls by its weight.

"Prayer," says Bloy, "is the work of free men, while work is the prayer of slaves." We are a great age for getting things done, having made a world of great cities and high buildings and large bridges and amazing systems of transportation and finances, yet what will it do for us if we have cast loose the spirit born in us, which has something to say? Even when this spirit is corrupted, it yearns for grandeur and expresses itself diabolically in Fascist and Nazi states. When it is corrupted in a materialistic society it yearns to possess limitless wealth. This spirit that hungers after the infinite and eternal and wants to hold conversation with God still trembles and yearns and agonizes in all things we do and seeks to have some satisfaction in communion. This is prayer, whether it be wordless, as in meditation; or in broken language; or in action done with full intent and spiritual imaginativeness.

Prayer is a thousand things, but it is always the meeting of God and man, and at that moment, there is peace that passeth all our understanding and joy that the world shall never take away. Lay up for yourselves treasures in the Spirit where moth and rust doth not corrupt and where thieves cannot break through nor steal, for where your treasure is, there your heart will find peace and joy and the fulfillment of all the anguish of your soul.

13

The Travail of Glory

MOST of us, at one time or another, have expressed the wish, vain as it may seem, to start life all over again. Looking back over our life and seeing what we have done to it, we sigh for a chance to redeem what we have so cheaply used or carelessly ruined. If only somehow, somewhere, there were a way to live again the days we have darkened with our blind haste—the innumerable occasions when our indifference trod on all the pearls of God's graciousness; the times when our pride, or our fear, or our meanness, poured the acid of our contempt over the fair countenance of another's soul—if this boon were ours, how we would leap to the chance!

But there is an even deeper yearning in this sigh of the soul to be born again. It is not that we futilely ask to be born at the beginning again, but rather that now being what we are, we are ill-content to go on in the same way. The past is past, and we know it. It cannot be broken or remade. There is no way back. Yet the past is not left in some forgotten limbo from which we have once and for all departed, leaving it all behind. It lies in the brain and the blood, in the habits of the mind and the skill of the hand, in the memory of the soul and the bonds of the spirit. The past is veritably present.

And this is our burden! Here in us, in these capacious hearts of ours, we carry strange peremptory devils who came to us in other days, came quietly and slowly at first with much courtesy and bright wit and enticing manners, but now that they are no longer casual guests but established members of our soul they act as masters and hold us to their will. Here in these hearts are the compromises we lightly made with the world, harmless and seemingly necessary ones at the time, but full of interminable and growing consequences. All of these we would like to repudiate, but habit being what it is, we will continue to the end of time, justifying ourselves with high-sounding but hollow phrases. Here in these hearts are the entanglements by which we have entered into social fellowship and become known by our fellows: all our opinions, our orthodoxy or our heresy, our party or our class or our set, our position or our profession or our reputation, everything which others have known or know about us, which they say or think we are. All these things are like stakes driven deeply into the earth and to which we have been tied—and who is there who will act out of character, do what is unexpected of him, dare to defy consistency of self or reputation among friends? Here in these hearts are the ruts —deep with many comings and goings, deep with the repeated patterns of many days and many nights, deep with the motion of our hands, the seeing of our eyes, the thinking of our minds, the desires of our hearts and the hopes of our souls—ruts made by knowledge as well as by ignorance, ruts of presumption, of hesitancy, of selfish security and of cowardly fear, of pride and of lust; deep, deep ruts made by half-truths, and half-lies, half-free and half-slave, half-life and half-death. This is the tangled network of all that we have ever thought or done in which the new life digs deeper the old ways.

These are the ruts, the entanglements, the compromises, the devils which bind us to what we have been and hold us from being what we want to be. We rise each day with new and courageous impulses, we daringly aim at a nobler and a more generous existence, we put all our energy back of it—and then scarcely has it moved when with a sickening thud it falls back into the well-worn rut of our habitual way of doing things. This is our tragedy, that with every new thing we try to do, with every attempt to live as we ought to live, with every desire to live differently, our life is so cut and scarred with what has gone before that it is difficult to move without falling to our accustomed level. Though we have new visions, our actions are old; though we have new experiences, our life follows the old routine; though we have new insights, our deeds and opinions are unchanged. This is our bitterness, that with all our better understanding as the years go by, we cannot seem to free ourselves from our own created habits. We have been tying ourselves with a million thoughts and as many separate acts, and now we can scarcely move except in the way in which the ropes command. What we want is not to start all over again—that is too idle a wish. We want rather to start now with a new life, free of the burden of this cursed giant of the past who towers in us; to begin a new life unhindered by the weight of all the acts and thoughts piled upon our backs by the years.

We know now the kind of life we would like to live; it is not the kind of life we are living; and the things that hold us from it are the spiritual habits, good, bad and indifferent, which we have built strongly by much practice. For me to be born again is to be born now, to start from where I am, to think and act and be as I have never been able to think and act and be. Yet "how shall a man be born when he is old?"

When, out of the pain of his soul, Nicodemus asked this anguished question, he spoke for us. With our lives growing more and more rigidly bound by the network of entanglements, by the pressure of our reputation and the persistence of habit, and by the momentum of routine, with innumerable days each lived in monotonous similarity, how can we start a new way? Having been born, how can we be born again? A day, or a year, or a score of years—what does it matter?—now that we are old, how shall we be born?

This imponderable load of precedent must have been heavy on Nicodemus. He was an educated man and, therefore, had cultural entanglements. He was a man of social prestige and, therefore, had certain duties expected of him. He was an orthodox Jew with the tradition of his race and of his family over his head. He had habits of judgment, habits of social opinion. How then could he be born again? You and I, very much like Nicodemus, with many good things to our credit, and a great many more that are merely passable, and more than we would care to admit that would never get under the bar, nevertheless have caught a glimpse of a kingdom, full of the grace and glory of God, abundant with the eternal spirit of creation. Of course our hearts are sore vexed with the narrow little alley of our traditional patterns of thought, our accustomed habits, our usual and casual action, our meager and often mean dimensions of life. But how shall Nicodemus the good Jew, and I the more or less Christian, be born out of our little darkness and squint-eyed existence into the infinite light and generous life of freedom in God?

The answer is short, direct and unmistakable. What is impossible with man, is possible with God. What seems to be so generally denied, is nevertheless often granted. All one can say is that these things happen, men are reborn, decisive changes are made and souls enter into new life. Men, in short, become new creations. Saul of Tarsus may be staked to an old pattern just as deeply and profoundly as Nicodemus. Trained as a Pharisee of the Pharisees, nurtured in a strict Jewish home, zealous of his faith to the point of fanaticism, achieving a brilliant and growing reputation—all these things in Saul of Tarsus made ruts of confining depth, and sanctified them with holy names and a religious passion. Yet Saul became Paul, and all the fiery passion that ran with irresistible energy through the old ruts of the law, now changed its course and its level, and ran through a new life of spirit. How can a man be born again?

This is all we know—men are born again! The stakes are pulled up, the compromises repudiated, the entanglements thrown off, the devils driven out, reputation denied, and with a leap life is started on a new level.

Obviously it is not altogether a pleasant experience. Travail is a necessity in the spiritual realm, just as in the physical, if there is to be birth. And if the new is to be achieved, something of the old must be discarded. Jacques Maritain says in "The Dark Night of Poetry":

> Each time the human mind puts itself to a different task, it begins its conquest of new fields and especially of its proper spiritual universe by bringing with all this a certain amount of disturbance, of disaster. The human being seems to become disorganized; and sometimes in fact it happens that crises of growth end unhappily. But there are, in any cases, *crises of growth*.*

Anyone that goes through life without

---

* *The Kenyon Review*, 1940.

encountering at some time the full power of his inherited and accustomed religion, and then and there does not enter into a merciless struggle to achieve a direct, immediate and personal "blessing" of insight, will go through the rest of his life woefully handicapped. That Jacob-struggle, the wrestling until the dawn of spirit-life comes, is the critical hour of our existence! Then one's soul rises in its own right and declares its absolute need of a spiritual relationship unhindered by what has gone before it. To put it briefly, there must be a beginning somewhere, when the soul with revolutionary decisiveness turns its attention to and places its interest in things of the spirit. As Jesus says, "That which is born of the flesh is flesh; that which is born of the spirit is spirit."

It is not enough to be born of flesh, for that is born to die. To fulfil our destiny we must also be born of the spirit, for that is to live eternally. To live carnally then is to live in death every day. To live carnally is not merely to live coarsely or lustfully or vulgarly. Carnal living is often the most respectable. It is, briefly, to live on the outside of everything, to judge all things, all persons and all occasions in terms of worldly advantage or pleasure or profit; it sees only appearance, reputation, traditions, and what men usually call happiness.

To live spiritually is to penetrate the "outsidedness" of life and find the treasure of God's riches at its heart. It is to leap beyond the ramparts of this world and to see it from the inside with understanding. It is to be conscious of the eternal stream of creation in God, and to know that there is no satisfaction of human thirst outside of it. "Be ye not conformed to this world," the apostle says, "but be ye transformed by the renewal of your mind"—in short, be born to this new and higher world. Soon or late, the yes-or-no decision must be given; one will have his treasures "here" or "there"; he will serve "mammon" or "God"—"either-or" but never both. Once that decision is made, the travail suffered, the new life entered, then the years may be full of creative occasions if a man has continuing sight to see them and continuing faith in the realm of the spirit to seek them above comfort and pride.

For a man's birth is not ended with the first gasp of his breath and the first cry of his lungs. He is born for innumerable births. He is forever pushing his way into new worlds. Through countless experiences, by high ecstasies and deep sorrows he plunges to new heights and depths in himself. Through the old symbols and new insights he sees fresh and alluring vistas. Grief and love lead him far beyond himself. Prophets and poets shout across the ages and call out his soul. Beauty unseals his eyes and reverence leads him to mystery and tenderness. The strange designs of circumstance and purpose, the impact of this world and all its wonders, the dark movings of the inner abyss in himself, all these are avenues of births beyond number.

Yet all of them shall be only pain and weariness of spirit unless in their midst one avenue is found where the door opens upon God and His realm. A burning bush for Moses, a cry in the night for Samuel, an unfaithful wife for Hosea, a potter's wheel for Jeremiah, a sanctuary vision for Ezekiel, a blinding light for Paul, a cross for Jesus—each finds his way and after that through all the devious windings of the spirit he drinks forever of the Holy Grail, the water of eternal life.

I have seen a tree made for the stage. Its leaves were paper and its trunk heavy cardboard. It could not grow and its leaves would not fall. As long as people were kept at a distance and dazzling lights of many colors played upon it, it looked very much like a tree. But the glory of a real tree was not in it. A true tree stands in the open field, rooted forever to one spot of earth, under the windy skies, enduring the fret of the rain and the drag of the wind. And its glory is manifest in its many deaths and many births. With every leaf filled with the majestic glory of the autumn, it casts them all to the wind and in naked poverty dies for the winter. Then the spring comes, and while the threat of snow and raw winds is still in the air, it puts forth its tender buds and in a miracle of mystery is born again. So through many years, dying and being born, again and again, it lives and fulfills its destiny.

If we really want to be born again, the sincerity of our desire will be known by the willingness with which we cast last season's leaves to the wind. There must be a lot of dying if there is to be any birth. The realm of the spirit is not to be gained without struggle and discipline and denial. "If any man will come after me, let him deny himself, and take up his cross." If any man decides to descend into the deeper levels of life or to climb to its heights, he must forego the crowded surface where the obvious is easily known or used for short-lived pleasure. The choice is essentially between the old wineskins and the new wine, between the forms of the past and the daring freedom of a deliberate purpose. It is the difference between Nicodemus and Paul, between radical conservatism and creative radicalism. Essentially it is the difference between life and death. To know that life, which is more than life, one must be born even though he is old. Conrad Aiken has indicated it magnificently:

> It is in that bravery, in that voluntary decision
> To walk forward into the darkness without vision,

To shape and know it violently, handle it
With hands unready but brave—in that always,
And every minute, and everywhere, and all our lives
Daring of the dark chasm, which, despite the sunlight,
And despite the flowers and the love and the grass,
And despite the bird song and the young song,
Lies just outside the heart; into this
Let us never cease to step gladly with terror;
For it is only in this that we shall avoid error,
Only in this speak suddenly the terrible word
Which is our birth and being and discovery and death in one,
The immortal speech that never before was heard.*

And so we stand again at the center of our weary hearts, asking the question, "How shall a man be born when he is old?" We want a new life, desperately—to be redeemed from unfortunate habits, frustrating fears, cowardly caution, prudent meanness, shallowness of mind and heart—but how shall it be accomplished, and when, and where, and by whom? Let Jesus speak the answer to us, as he spoke it to Nicodemus: "The wind bloweth where it listeth, and thou hearest the sound thereof, but canst not tell whence it cometh, and whither it goeth." Two women shall be grinding corn, it taketh one and leaveth one. Two men shall be in the field, it taketh one and leaveth one. The election of the soul is in the mysteries of God's grace.

But do not despair! Do not throw up your hands and deliver over your soul to death. Do not strike a bargain even with the best of devils for the sake of petty peace. Remember, say it aloud, repeat it in your prayers, cry aloud before God and besiege Him night and day—He who hungers and thirsts after righteousness shall be filled. The meek shall inherit the kingdom of God. The pure in heart shall see God. He who is persecuted in the name of religion, shall rejoice. He who knocks, to him shall it be opened; who seeketh, findeth; who asketh, receiveth an answer.

Into our yearning, into the agony of desire, into the empty loneliness of our souls, the grace of God will pour its streams of golden light until it seems as though the very stones must shout in joy if we withhold a syllable of humble praise glorified by this new life. And all our days we will know a new heaven and a new earth. We will know the old world to be only the husk of the kingdom's glory, without sustenance or satisfaction.

A man may be born again, yes, a man must be born again—not by the will of man nor by the will of the flesh, but by the will of God. Let us, therefore, surrender to His grace, that we may lay ourselves away and become new creations in Christ Jesus, co-heirs with him of all the unfathomable riches of the Eternal.

---

* Conrad Aiken, *The Going Forth*. *Harper's magazine*, Nov., 1939. Copyright, 1939, by Conrad Aiken, and used by permission of the author.

14

The Inevitable Cross

THE Cross is a vast, persistent, monumental fact as fundamentally mysterious as anything in the whole broad field of religion. If we could come to it with an unaccustomed mind and heart, and see it freshly for the first time, I suspect we would be utterly astonished that such a thing as a cross on which a man had died in great agony and considerable shame should be elevated as one of the affirmations of religious faith. We would impulsively ask, "What in the world can this mean? Towering o'er the wrecks of time, as it does, persisting beyond the collapse of many different philosophies of life, enduring in spite of catastrophes of history, why do multitudes of men and women continue to believe in it, to assert that it has some strange significance in the meaning of human existence?" Obviously there is something *in man* which gives meaning to the Cross, and it is equally plain that there is something *in God* which gives an ultimate meaning to this particular Cross.

It is true that we are forced to admit that the symbol itself is appropriated by multitudes of people who do not have either the knowledge or the courage to practice the way of life which it indicates. We can easily understand why Orozco, the Mexican artist, depicted a towering cross against a brilliant sky, and at its base, the Lord of Wrath, the Mighty One Himself, the very one who had given it meaning originally by his own suffering and death, standing with an ax and hewing it down as if it had lost its usefulness in developing the experience and deepening the life of mankind. It is possible for the Cross to become a trinket, or, even worse than that, to become an obstruction rather than a liberating mystery of deep and prolific power. To misunderstand it, or not to understand it at all; to misuse it, or to accept it without practicing its way of life, will be to make it an offense in the eyes of him who hung upon it.

In exploring, then, the meaning of this

Christian Cross, one will quickly see that it must be understood in the light of that early controversy between Christ and his disciples. You will remember that when he mentioned it to them, they were so amazed that it can only be deduced that they thought it to be foreign to God's blessing. For them, as for most Jews of their time, the beatitudes of God excluded the possibility of pain. It was Peter who as much as said, "Far be it from Thee, Lord, to go up to Jerusalem and suffer death. If thou art the Chosen One, favored of God, then neither pain nor suffering can come nigh unto thee."

That is not a strange doctrine. It is identically the same doctrine which has taken hold of our own modern world in which we feel that suffering is to be eliminated from life as quickly and as completely as possible. In fact, a great deal of our activity not only seeks to eliminate any uncomfortable elements from the world, but we do all we can to avoid any inconvenience. We try to make life a smooth road, to make existence comfortable, and to make our lives as pleasant and pleasurable as we can.

Surely this is quite human, and yet there is a danger, as E. Stanley Jones once said, of taking the crucifix out of the church and replacing it with nothing more than cushions. It is little wonder that for multitudes of comfort-loving Christians the Cross has become scarcely more than a lovely trinket or an ecclesiastical decoration. It is difficult for us to assume that suffering has a place in the economy of God for the blessing of man. But if the Cross is to remain at the center of Christianity, I can find no other meaning for it. We are saying that the final beatitude of man and the most adequate philosophy of his life must include suffering in some fundamental fashion, and not seek to escape it.

There are people in this world who find some peculiar self-satisfaction in suffering, and who will find reasons for martyrdom with the slightest provocation. This was not what Jesus was talking about. There is no indication that he had any pathological love of suffering for its own sake. And wherever Christianity has wallowed in the self-infliction of pain, it has departed from the spirit and the way of the Master. To

Jesus, the Cross was pain and agony, not a sentimental fascination.

We can see something of the mystery of this matter by observing that as soon as a man begins to avoid all pain or suffering, to escape from it at all costs and to make his life as pleasant and pleasurable as he can, he runs inevitably into a world of unreality, in which there is neither height nor depth to his existence. It becomes as light as froth which the wind blows away.

No character in literature illustrates as well this fact of life as Tito in George Eliot's *Romola*. As Romola holds little Lillo's face in her hands, she says to him:

> There was a man to whom I was very near, so that I could see a great deal of his life, who made almost everyone fond of him, for he was young, and clever, and beautiful, and his manners to all were gentle and kind. I believe when I first knew him, he never thought of anything cruel or base. But because he tried to slip away from everything that was unpleasant and cared for nothing else as much as his own safety, he came at last to commit some of the basest

deeds—such as make men infamous. He denied his father, and left him to misery; he betrayed every trust that was reposed in him, that he might keep himself safe and get rich and prosperous. Yet calamity overtook him.

It is as if suffering is one of the characteristics by which life is made abundant and meaningful, and once we get out of this height and depth we live on a superficial surface where there is actually no substance or weight to experience itself. Somehow or other suffering turns us back to a fuller, richer, more vibrant and vital living. When a minister walks into a house where death has called, he sees people deeply and fundamentally alive in the presence of this profoundest and most painful mystery of our existence. Within a day or a week they will once again move out of this depth of essential dignity, out upon the superficial aspects of this great and restless world of ours, and what they were at their best in the cryptic presence of death will be hidden by the amiable courtesies that mean so little and fill so much of time and life.

In the second place, the Christian Cross is to be understood in terms of Christ's serious devotion to God. It is not easy to indicate the kind of profound seriousness with which Jesus thought of God. It did not exclude joy as so much of our seriousness does. Nor was it the mood of a moment, as befalls us from time to time. It was the kind of seriousness that bluntly and, I am afraid, somewhat impudently, replied to his mother when he was twelve that he must be about his Father's business; or that forgave people in spite of the fact that he knew his reputation was going to be bad from that time on. When he preached his gospel in Nazareth, he preached the good news of God's unlimited graciousness to all men, although he knew that the Jews, so inordinately proud of themselves, would never forgive him. When he set his face to go to Jerusalem, and to confront the vast structure of pomp and pride both of the temple and of the state, he knew that he would lose his disciples, yet he did not hesitate to do what he believed to be his Father's will. Wherever you put your finger on events in the life of Jesus, you will find him extremely faithful to God—so faithful that whenever doing God's will involved considerable loss of face before men or loss of comfort to himself or even the threat of crucifixion with its criminal stain of shame and its mortal agony, he preferred to be counted among the transgressors rather than to save himself, for it would have lost him God.

It is hard to see any possibility of any man at any time seriously trying to do the will of God, if he is forever keeping an eye on what the world thinks about it, or what he will get out of it, or what consequences will descend upon him after he does it. The Cross is actually the measure of the world's resistance to the will of God. It is an indication that man is often God's worst enemy, and at the same time that one man, if he be single-hearted, is stronger than the whole world.

The third thing about the Christian Cross is that it seems to be involved in the peculiar difference between the Pharisees' life and that of Jesus. The Pharisees were extremely self-concerned. They took themselves very seriously indeed. They were anxious about their righteousness and tremendously zealous about the petty minutiae of their laws. Jesus, on the other hand, was not self-concerned. Indeed, it is difficult from the records in the Synoptic Gospels for even the best of scholars to determine what Jesus thought about himself. If there were not an unfortunate connotation about the word "nonchalance," one might say that Jesus was nonchalant. Again, this does not exclude his seriousness before God, but, being serious before God, he could be, in a sense, nonchalant with men. Not that he took men less seriously but having faith in God, he was not tortured into feeling uneasy about them. He was not tempted, therefore, to use the coercive methods and regulative controls of the Pharisees to keep men within decent bounds. There is a sense of relaxation and peace and poise about Jesus. "Take no thought for the morrow," he says; "are there not twelve hours in the day?" It is as if he said: "Respect the peace and life of this day and surrender completely to its needs, not exhausting one's strength by fears for the morrow, but knowing that each day has its own strength and its own responsibilities."

Fundamentally, the Pharisees killed their souls by their extreme self-concern. The more they grew anxious of their reputation and prestige, the more petty and fearful and bitter they became. One remembers Sandburg's little phrase, "Beware of the little death," for the fate of the Pharisees was to die the little death. Jesus lost his life, it is true, but it was lost in such a magnitude of purpose, in such spaciousness of meaning and peace, that it became the "great death," a death of such greatness that in it men saw an open door to the victory of a new kind of life. How much better to die the great death of the Christian Cross than the little death of petty concern.

Finally, we must say of this Christian Cross that through it we have a peculiar sense of Jesus' dying for us. This is not intellectually demonstrable but strangely enough it is spiritually available as a real experience. Somehow we feel that we were involved in that crucifixion. Being part of humanity, we are involved in the sin that made it possible. The forces that crucified Jesus are not foreign to our souls or to the way in which we live. They were respectable Pharisees protecting the tradition of their faith; they were officers of the state, administering as well as they could law and order; they were a frenzied crowd; and all these things we have been in our time. It is not hard to see that, in a sense, humanity made the Cross necessary then and even now makes it equally necessary for multitudes of our fellow beings. This is the sad burden we bear today, for we cannot isolate ourselves from responsibility for the tragedies that overtake the rest of the world.

If this be true, we also feel that the man on the Cross suffered for us and freed us by his death. He, too, is part of our humanity, and yet in him was a mystery of God we cannot explain, and in his suffering a peculiar beatitude that frees us from our guilt and shame and fear of death. I do not know how these things are, or how they came about, but I do know that in the Cross there is the revelation of a larger dimension to life's meaning by which our souls are liberated and find their peace.

This Christian Cross stretches into the darkness and the light of God and its roots descend into the darkness and the light of our own depth. It is something that has grown out of us and if it had never come into being as a symbol of Christianity, you and I would have been forced to search for something in order to picture to ourselves this profoundly deep and significant experience of our human order. There is no need for us to take up the Cross in one sense, for it was already a portion of us when we were born into humanity, incarnate in the flesh, and subject to the law of the flesh. It is our humanity, with its inevitable embarrassment and guilt and sorrow—things not to be avoided, regardless of our sophistication or intelligence. For this Cross is a life which must be lived with all its hope of eternal significance and day-by-day futility, wherein both the dream and the deed will be darkened not only by our failure, but by the cruelty of a resisting and belligerent world. There is no other way than to accept it, take it up and carry it humbly and with all the spiritual resources of the faith we may be able to achieve in such a world.

If we shake ourselves loose from it as though it did not belong to us, and turn our backs upon it, we will commit the most unreal of all unrealities and become as weak as any other shadow. We shall find ourselves veritable empty houses—mere walls around an inner vacuum, a series of unsustaining and meaningless experiences. Jesus never said, "Fondle the cross," but he did say, "If any man will come after me, let him deny himself, and take up his cross, and follow me." Mysteriously enough, there is some kind of blessing which we will not get except in carrying it.

15

Beginning Eternity Now

MULTITUDES keep Easter for no other reason than that springtime stirs their soul in some vague and nameless way associated with religion. Long before Christ came, however, men were deeply moved by this annual miracle of the earth, and responded to it with all kinds of rites. The celebration of Easter merely as a festival of earth's renewal is scarcely Christian. Essentially it is pagan, an obviously religious, pagan experience.

There is something much more profound and significant about the Christian Easter than the pleasurable return of warm weather in the world. The fact that there will be new flowers and lovely trees, and a riotous out-burst of beauty across the earth will scarcely answer the distressing problems of our day, the threat to international peace, and the abiding fears and anxieties of man's heart. If

Easter has a meaning in the Christian sense, it must confront the grief and tragic need within the very heart of man.

There is a sense in which we begin eternity here and now. It is not something that we will easily add on to the end of life when we die. It is not merely a heaven of golden streets and angels playing harps in a realm of endless joy. These are spiritual caricatures of the Christian truth about eternity. Certainly no man knew more about this mystery of life and death, of heaven and hell, and eternity than the apostle Paul, and this is what he said, "I count everything loss for the excellency of Christ Jesus my Lord. . . . That I may know him and the power of his resurrection, and the fellowship of his sufferings, being made conformable with his death, if by any means I might attain to the resurrection of the dead. Not as if I had already attained, or were made perfect." It was not a guaranteed thing; it was not the sure and certain solution to all the problems neglected here on earth. For Paul there was a perilous sense that the soul might be lost, and eternity never gained. There was a chance that no matter how many times the earth had revolved in its orbit, and springtime had broken in grandeur, man alone in all this reborn creation might say No to his own soul, and refusing to be born again, choose to go down, damned to extinction by death! Somehow or other in the development of later Christendom, we have taken out of Christianity this peril or risk, and have come to feel very tolerant and comfortable, as though every soul, regardless of its self-neglect or self-destructiveness, will come at last to have heaven dropped into its undeserving hands. This belief is not in the New Testament.

Fundamentally, the Christian meaning of Easter would imply that eternity has something to do with our way of life now. It has something to do with all the casual, ordinary circumstances that fill our days and nights, year after year, long before death comes to call upon us. It is not something that is started suddenly when the body breathes its last breath, but is part of our very breathing now. Jesus put the matter very pointedly in the story of the wise and foolish virgins. There would be some who would be ready when the bridegroom came, for their lamps would have been already filled with oil, and there would be others who would not be ready to enter the festive joy of the wedding because their lamps had been left empty. This is not a vague story. He did not say, "When death arrives, hurry and search for whatever you can find to help you." He was saying that when the hour comes, our work should have prepared us for it. If there is no oil in the lamps, it will be too late to borrow it or to steal it, for these treasures, laid up in heaven, are not like the treasures we lay up on earth where in an emergency we can exchange or borrow or steal. These spiritual treasures we must have ourselves or we will not have them any other way, and cannot get them from anyone.

It is just as if a man should say, "I have been playing tennis now for forty years. Next Tuesday afternoon I shall pick up a violin and start playing Brahm's Violin Concerto." We would laugh at him and say, "What a fool you are! You have not prepared yourself for playing the violin, but for playing tennis." How ridiculous it is of us to assume we can enjoy fellowship with God after we die, while all our lives we have been avoiding His fellowship. To spend time with God when we have not prepared ourselves for it, will be equivalent to spending time in hell.

There is in life itself, this life which we live from day to day, something of a heaven and a hell in every occasion. It is not as if we needed to wait until the end of time and then tack heaven or hell on to it. Actually, there are three levels here: a lower level where life is denied and destroyed; a middle level where life is merely lived without much thought or meaning, a bare existence, although it may be luxurious with wealth and pleasure; and a third level full of rich and significant meanings in which satisfaction is lasting and life is eternal. The first is obviously hell, the second is nothing more than the world, and the third is really heaven. The man who actually prepares for what happens after death is he who knows that there is a hell and a heaven potentially in each occasion, and, therefore, he gives himself to fulfill the possibility of heaven involved in the circumstances of his day. He releases and completes in himself with

God's help the eternal reality of the temporal world. This is what I mean by saying that eternity must begin now for it is part of our human life.

The second thing about eternity is that it has implications for our normal everyday life in the sense that it is tied up with death, and death itself is not a thing that comes merely at the end of life. Time is the little death that comes day after day, week after week. It creeps on with petty pace, taking from us a strength of body, clarity of mind, and in due time our very breath. Time is a little death—the shadow cast before the great and formidable death—and if we do not learn how to conquer this little death of time in which we live and move and have our being, how shall we conquer that most formidable death that waits for us at the end our pilgrimage? Eternity begins now, wherever and whenever we triumph over the death of time and lift ourselves above its denial and slow destructiveness to a spiritual life where we fulfill the designs and purposes of God for any hour or any person.

Make no mistake about it, we die day after day whether we want to die or not.

The question is whether we will confront these little deaths day after day and merely die in dying, or be resurrected by those deaths to a larger life in God and in His purposes. Where there is no death, there is no resurrection; where there is no transcendence over this lower level of life, there is no path into eternity; where there is no Good Friday or pain of travail, there is no Easter. Eternity begins whenever and wherever we are able to transcend the present dimensions of our living to become greater and larger souls. This is the very will of God, the very nature of being a soul, the very way by which the soul manifests itself in the world! Unless it grows it is dead. This is indicated in the strange symbol of the phoenix so universally acknowledged in literature. This is the legendary bird forever destroyed in flame only to be reborn from its ashes. This persistent myth repeats the doctrine that there is no life except by the conquest of death. Eternity is not a vague, far-off possibility but the most intimate and immediate problem of everyday life.

It is plain that if eternity is so intimately associated with the practice of life it introduces us to a constant crisis. Once a man has discovered that there are realms of the spirit which he can reach even here and now by his refusal to be satisfied with the meager dimensions of the world of appearance and reputation, he finds himself in a warfare which is unremitting. The confining limits of worldly existence which seemed to be the very essence of comfort now are revealed as too narrow for the expression of his life and spirit. What can be his without any trouble now looks like a poor and mean escape from what he may be even though it can be accomplished only with suffering and travail of spirit. He is now initiated into the warfare of the eternal spirit.

When Michelangelo was asked to paint the great ceilings of the Sistine Chapel, he could have repeated what he had painted so competently in many places before. However, this was the call for his genius to be reborn in larger and more magnificent dimensions than anything his art had suggested up to that time. To his great and lasting glory it must be said that his soul was great enough to become greater than it had been. No one can enter the kingdom of God where there are always new and increasing dimensions of life unless they are willing to be born again and again.

Eternity is mixed invisibly with the stuff of this earth. With every new coming of springtime across the earth, some men will continue to live the old, old life they have always lived while others will see that most amazing stuff we call the soul that shines with potential surprises able to begin again no matter how far it has gone, stretching itself toward that peace which is only known in the endless dimensions of God's eternal purpose. Every man, if he lifts his head far enough into life and out of the mere world of appearance, will discover that he is a child of God, not by some peculiar magic of the strange gift of the Church, but because there has been invested in him the ability to transcend himself again and again so that when the formidable death of the body comes he has no fear of it. He has been born and reborn so many times; he has laughed through the little deaths of little days so that now at the coming of this great death he is unmoved. Death is no stranger. He has prepared for himself a peace, a laying up of heavenly treasures so that he need not fear and need not wait, for in his own hand there is the answer to this deep and abiding darkness that dwells within his bones.

THE END

Large Print Inspirational Books from Walker

Would you like to be on our Large Print mailing list?
Please send your name and address to:

B. Walker
Walker and Company
720 Fifth Avenue
New York, NY 10019

Among available titles are:

The Prophet
Kahlil Gibran

Gift from the Sea
Ann Morrow Lindbergh

The Power of Positive Thinking
Norman Vincent Peale

Words to Love by
Mother Teresa

A Gathering of Hope
Helen Hayes

Woman to Woman
Eugenia Price

The Burden is Light
Eugenia Price

Apples of Gold
Jo Petty

Getting Through the Night: Finding Your Way After the Loss of a Loved One
Eugenia Price

The Genesee Diary:
Report from a
Trappist Monastery
Henri J. M. Nouwen

God in the Hard Times
Dale Evans Rogers

A Grief Observed
C. S. Lewis

He Began with Eve
Joyce Landorf

Hinds' Feet on High Places
Hannah Hurnard

Hope and Faith for Tough Times
Robert H. Schuller

Irregular People
Joyce Landorf

Jonathan Livingston Seagull
Richard Bach

The Little Flowers of Saint Francis of Assisi
Illustrated with woodcuts

No Man Is an Island
Thomas Merton

Reflections on the Pslams
C. S. Lewis

The Road Less Traveled: A New Psychology of Love, Traditional Values and Spiritual Growth
M. Scott Peck, M.D.

The Sacred Journey
Frederick Buechner

The Secret Kingdom
Pat Robertson

The Seven Storey Mountain
Thomas Merton

**Surprised by Joy
The Shape of My Early Life**
C. S. Lewis

Something Beautiful for God:
Mother
Teresa of Calcutta
Malcolm Muggeridge

Not I, But Christ
Corrie ten Boom

Out of Solitude
Henri J. M. Nouwen

Peace With God
Billy Graham

The Practice of the Presence of God
Brother Lawrence
Introduction by Dorothy Day

**Prayers and Promises for Every Day
From the Living Bible**
with Corrie Ten Boom

Reaching Out
Henri J. M. Nouwen

Abraham Lincoln: A Spiritual Biography
Elton Trueblood

The Day Christ Was Born
Jim Bishop

Enjoy the Lord
Father John Catoir

God Cares for You
Richard Dayringer

Golden Treasury of Psalms and Prayers
Selected by Edna Beilenson

Handel's Messiah: A Devotional Commentary
Joseph McCabe

The Life of the Soul
Samuel Miller

Teach Me to Pray
Gabe Huck

When the Well Runs Dry
Thomas H. Green, S.J.

The Adventure of Spiritual Healing
Michael Drury

The Alphabet of Grace
Frederick Buechner

A Book of Hours
Elizabeth Yates

Beginning to Pray
Anthony Bloom

A Certain Life: Contemporary Meditations on the Way of Christ
Herbert O'Driscoll

The Christian Faith
David H. C. Read

A Diary of Private Prayer
John Baillie

Fear No Evil
David Watson